PRAISE FOR EYE OF THE STORM

"Ray Williams's book combines practical mindfulness insights with powerful leadership techniques based on both experience and a thorough review of the research literature." -- Emma Seppälä, Ph.D, Associate Director Center for Compassion and Altruism Research and Education Stanford University School of Medicine

"Eye of the Storm is a compelling look at the failure of management to engage its workforce in meaningful work. Author Ray Williams neatly dissects the problem and offers solutions. Each is rooted in mindfulness, the sense of being in the moment as well as fully engaged with others. Williams offers tactical approaches for the readers that are specific and actionable. Eye of the Storm is a good read that belongs on the shelves of leaders everywhere."--John Baldoni, internationally acclaimed thought leader, executive coach and author of many books on leadership including MOXIE: The Secret to Bold and Gutsy Leadership

"Ray Williams provides a powerful narrative that explains why the workplace is such a toxic environment for all employees, and then gives real actionable solutions to turn your ship away from the storm and into paradise. You'll learn why mindful leadership is the best management style for increasing engagement, and morale, with your employees—which will not only make your job easier, but allow you sleep better at night."—Dan Schawbel, New York Times best selling author of Promote Yourself and Founder of WorkplaceTrends.com

"Eye of the Storm shows you how to create an environment where people are happy, creative, productive and look forward to getting to work each day."--Brian Tracy, Internationally renowned personal and professional achievement expert, speaker, thought leader and author of his new book How the Best Leaders Lead

"The practice of mindfulness is now spreading to many organizations as a practical strategy for employee well-being. Ray Williams's book describes in detail those practices and their benefits as a strategic way of responding to stress and lack of employee engagement. Ray's book also argues convincingly how mindful leaders can make a major impact on their organizations. Readers will find this book a valuable resource in change management and workplace culture initiatives."-- Dr. Tony Alessandra, author of The NEW Art of Managing People and The Platinum Rule

"Ray Williams documents and confirms the current dysfunctional and toxic condition of our corporations and the leaders who serve them. Ray provides a refreshing and frank review of not only what got us here - but what we need to do to fix it. The evidence presented in this book is irrefutable - that if we are to succeed our leadership culture, style, and practices MUST change and change now! This book is for every leader who desires a roadmap to success." --Ken Keis, PhD., President & CEO Consulting Resource Group, Co-Author Deliberate Leadership Creating Success Through Style

"Ray Williams does a masterful job of connecting the current global demographic, philosophical, and sociological changes that are taking place in our work environment with what that means for leaders today. He shares the practical tools and techniques of mindfulness to help leaders reimagine, rethink, and put to action the behaviors and habits necessary to truly be effective and successful in the fast-paced, ever-changing, highly competitive world we live in. As a leader if you have come to a place in your life where you realize that the pace you're working and living at is just not sustainable, or you're just curious to know how mindfulness can play a part in helping you live a life that is more on-purpose, then this is the book for you." - Mike Desjardins, CEO, VIRTUS INC.

"Eye of the Storm is both powerful and helpful today as executives are bombarded with constant messages, calls and requests for decisions. Williams's advice on how leaders need to capture a moment to pause; to reflect; calm the distractions; and become more mindful is excellent. He has done a great job outlining the challenges and opportunities today with leadership and how 'knowing thyself' is critical to success."—Brian Conlin, Global CEO, Golder Associates Corp.

Eye of the Storm: How Mindful Leaders Can Transform Chaotic Workplaces

Ray Williams

Ray Williams Associates
#1803-499 Broughton Street,
Vancouver BC V6G 3K1
Canada

Cover Design by Natalie Kathleen.

DEDICATION

This book is dedicated to Diane Williams for her unending support, encouragement and inspiration.

CONTENTS

ACKNOWLEDGMENTS

I've been fortunate to receive the sage advice and assistance of a number of individuals who assisted me in the research and preparation of this book. No achievement is ever the result of one single individual. I would like to thank Diane Williams for her tireless work as my editor. Natalie Kathleen devoted countless hours in the cover and interior designs of the book, for which I am truly grateful. And I appreciate the time that those professionals spent reviewing my book and providing testimonials: Brian Tracy, Emma Seppälä, Marshall Goldsmith, Ken Keis, Brian Conlin, Michael Webb, Dan Schawbel, Mike Desjardins, Tony Alessandra, John Baldoni, Robin Hemmingsen and James Kouzes.

PREFACE

"Two roads diverged in a wood, and I—I took the one less travelled by, and that has made all the difference."—Robert Frost

During the last two decades, I've had the privilege of working as an Executive Coach and Consultant with CEOs, senior executives, HR professionals and middle managers in Fortune 500 companies, Best Managed Companies in Canada, and other large, medium-sized and small firms, including startups. I've worked both with public sector organizations and those in the private sector. That work has been greatly rewarding and given me an insight how organizations work and the nature of the people who lead them.

During that time, I've been struck by the wide differences that exist among organizations in terms of their organizational culture, leadership style and employee behavior and relationships.

Some organizations can be characterized as being chaotic, unfriendly and rife with conflict and a malaise, almost palatable when you walk in the door. Leaders in the organization are not trusted; there is high turnover and absenteeism; and productivity, worker engagement and well-being are low.

Other organizations were clearly different. They were vibrant, friendly places, where respect and trust for leaders was clearly evident. And most employees are long-term, cooperative; and their engagement, productivity and well-being levels are high. It was like Charles Dickens' *Tale of Two Cities*. Over the years, I'd seen many leaders, management consultants, trainers, reorganizations, and flavor of the month workshops come and go--often with little effect on dysfunctional organizations.

Which led me to examine in depth the "why" of what made great organizations and the nature of their leaders. Of course, much has been written about this by management experts such as Tom Peters and Jim Collins. And the organizations they examined and leadership styles that were espoused, quite frankly seemed to have a shelf life.

Coincidentally with finding the answer to that question, I became immersed personally and professionally in the growing interest and research on mindfulness, which happened to fit perfectly with my approach to coaching executives, which is very much an "inside-out" process.

So this book is both an effort to define and describe the disheartening and dysfunctional state of the workplace, and also examine the mindfulness phenomena as it applies to leadership and the workplace.

It is my hope that leaders and professionals will be able to use the book and the resources contained within as a stimulus for discussion, and potential changes in organizations. At the end of each chapter I've provided some links for readers to follow up that will provide more practical strategies for implementation.

There is a fork in the road. And we need, more than ever, to take the mindful one.

Ray Williams
Vancouver
April, 2015

INTRODUCTION BY MARSHALL GOLDSMITH

In Eye of the Storm, you'll learn what's really happening in the workforce as new generations supplant the old; how to turn around a toxic workplace; and the critical difference between doing and being.

Ray Williams analyzes the seismic shifts taking place in the foundation of the global workplace. He persuasively argues that that the workplace structures and culture that we know now are morphing right under our feet, and companies must adapt new perspectives and practices or risk imminent failure.

Eye of the Storm is thoroughly researched. Any leader, especially those who are striving to implement change at work, will benefit from this provocative and pragmatic book. The book will be especially helpful to those working in a broken environment. *Eye of the Storm* will be your salvation.

Marshall Goldsmith is recognized as one of the top ten Most Influential Business Thinkers in the world, and author of the best selling books, *What Got You Here, Won't Get You There, MOJO, Coaching for Leadership and Succession: Are You Ready?* and his new book, *Triggers: Creating Behavior That Lasts--Becoming the Person You Want to Be.*

1 THE STORM IN THE WORKPLACE

Despite the advances of progressive organizations and their leaders, the storm in the current workplace is a reflection of a dysfunctional and obsolete model of business and toxic working conditions for employees.

For more than the past two decades, I have been engaged in coaching and training leaders in organizations and mentoring young aspiring leaders. During that time, I've had the opportunity to go into organizations -- private and public -- and experience first hand, their culture, leadership styles, employee relationships and product and service results. My experience has been the tale of two cities. In some organizations, it was immediately apparent from the positive and cooperative attitudes of leaders and their staff, and their relationships with vendors and customers, that something exceptionally good was happening there, and my presence there was just part of the strategy to get even better. The other city, the darker one, unfortunately far too common, was characterized by a heavy malaise, lethargy, unhappy employees and conflict and mistrust with management. My presence there was seen more as remedial work with leaders, and other employees.

The question for me that I wrestled with, what was the difference? And what accounted for or could account for the difference? And that prompted me to write this book, to examine the whys and suggest a way of addressing the issues.

The Toxic Corporation
Corporations were invented to organize large numbers of workers in single locations to complete mostly automated tasks. In this world of business, enlightened self-interest of business owners was sufficient to ensure

economic progress. But one hundred years later, this simple arrangement is now antiquated. A new way of organizing work and allocating resources for more complex and rapidly changing work is needed.

In *The Corporation*, the hit 2003 documentary film, businesses are portrayed as psychopaths that can wreak havoc in the communities where they operate, something that is becoming increasingly commonplace.

Relentless demands, extreme pressure and brutal ruthlessness are all trademarks of a toxic company, as is a twisted disconnect between what a firm says it does for employees and what it actually is doing. People are looked at as costs, rather than assets. On its books, a company might have progressive policies regarding work-life issues, but in fact employs part-time workers, who are struggling to balance career and family. Fear and paranoia, and anxiety to the point of panic, are other characteristics of a toxic workplace.

"You can tell as soon as you walk into an office that it's toxic," says Barbara Moses, a consultant in career management and author of *What Next? The Complete Guide to Taking Control of Your Working Life*, among other employment-related books. "People are rushed; they have that harried look," she says, "Conversations are curt and abrupt; there's no chance for thoughtful, rich conversation."

There are multiple reasons why the toxic workplace is proliferating. With mega-mergers and globalization, some corporations are becoming more vast and impersonal, while simultaneously recurring waves of job cuts have left companies lean and left individuals with workloads greater than is reasonably feasible over the long haul. Instead of rewarding long-term planning, expediency is demanded.

Add in a leader who ignores the human toll, and the result is likely a toxic workplace. Creative and innovative ideas--ironically, the factors that drive the best corporations -- are stifled; employees are alienated; people get sick.

According to Jeffrey Pfeffer, American business theorist and the Thomas D. Dee II Professor of Organizational Behavior at the Graduate School of Business, Stanford University, when it comes to the link between people and profits, companies get exactly what they deserve.

Companies that treat their people right get enormous dividends--high rates of productivity, and low rates of turnover. Companies that treat their people poorly experience the opposite -- and end up complaining about the

death of loyalty and the dearth of talent. These are "toxic work,
according to Pfeffer, the author of *The Human Equation: Building .
Putting People First* .

Pfeffer disputes much of the conventional wisdom in the current
conversation about work and business. Loyalty isn't dead, he insists but
toxic companies are driving people away. There isn't a scarcity of talent --
but there is a growing unwillingness to work for toxic organizations. Pfeffer
also disputes the idea of the end of the career. "I don't believe that people
are looking to go flitting from one job to the next," he says. "People are
looking for the opportunity to have variety in their work and to tackle
challenging assignments. The best companies are figuring out how their
employees can have both opportunities -- without leaving."

Pfeffer says, "It mystifies me that so many companies think they can get a
cheap competitive advantage by purchasing something on the open market!
Anything that you can purchase on the open market is also available to your
competitors. So the question is, how can you distinguish yourself in a world
in which your competitors can copy everything you do? The answer is, all
that separates you from your competitors are the skills, knowledge,
commitment, and abilities of the people who work for you. There is a very
compelling business case for this idea: Companies that manage people right
will outperform companies that don't by 30% to 40%." This principle,
Pfeffer argues, even applies to the current IPO market: IPO firms that
value their people have a much higher five-year survival rate than those that
don't.

Similar studies of the steel industry, the oil-refining industry, the apparel
industry, and the semiconductor industry all demonstrate the enormous
productivity benefits that come with implementing high-performance, high-
involvement management practices.

Pfeffer contends companies have killed loyalty by becoming toxic places to
work. Start with the interviewing and recruiting process. What happens on a
new employee's first day in a company with no employees' union? The
company asks the employee to sign an at-will employment contract that
gives the company the right to fire the person at any time and for any
reason. What message is being sent?

Another sign that a company is toxic: It requires people to choose between
having a life and having a career. A toxic company says to people, "We
want to own you." There's an old joke that they used to tell about working
at Microsoft: "We offer flexible time -- you can work any 18 hours you

want."

A toxic company says, "We're going to put you in a situation where you have to work in a style and on a pace that is not sustainable. We want you to come in here and burn yourself out -- and then you can leave." Another sign of a toxic workplace, Pfeffer argues, is that the company treats its people as if they were a factors of production. At a toxic workplace, the managers can reel off all of the various economic factors such as: "We've got capital that we invest, we've got raw material that we use, we've got the waste from the manufacturing process that we recycle -- and, in the same category, we've got our people." It's a workplace that doesn't see people as people, but rather sees them as factors of production. And that's ironic, because what we celebrate as a competitive, capitalistic practice actually reflects a Marxist orientation: People are seen as a factor of production, from which a company has to extract an economic "surplus."

In one of the companies that I was brought into work as a coach, I was struck by the nature of the language of the leaders and the Board of Directors. A sanitized jargon that referred to employees as expenditures or costs without reference to them as human beings dominated the briefings and discussions, and rarely did I hear employees referred to as assets or in terms of being human. The focus of attention in executive meetings was often spreadsheets, statistics and reports, but a discussion about how people in the organization were feeling and thinking about their work rarely arose.

The Failure of Management As We Know It
An increasing number of management experts see a clear connection between the dysfunctions of the current workplace and the development of Western style capitalism during the last century, one that has almost exclusively focused on shareholder value and financial profits. Here's a sample of the voices questioning this fundamental proposition:

- Clayton Christensen and Derek van Bever, writing in *Harvard Business Review,* contend "The orthodoxies governing finance are so entrenched that we almost need a modern-day Martin Luther to articulate the need for change."
- Gautam Mukanda also writing in the *Harvard Business Review*, points to the "excessive financialization" of the economy and the unbalanced power of the financial sector over sound management mindsets. Executives are making choices they know are wrong."

- Roger Martin, writing in the *Harvard Business Review*, argues "The move to building value to trading value is bad for economic growth and performance. Talent is being channeled into unproductive activities and egregious behaviors."

We have yet to come to terms with the fact that the old way of doing work and business no longer is functional. Free market capitalism has failed us. Angel Guria, Secretary General for the OECD argues: "We failed as regulators, we failed as supervisors, we failed as corporate managers, we failed as risks mangers and we also failed in the allocation of roles and responsibilities for international economic organizations." Referring to the current model of capitalism and business, Guria says "The game is over and we need a fundamental restructuring –essentially about how people will live, and we need to move beyond simple notions about growth to more sophisticated, nuanced discussions about human progress."

Sara Robinson, writing in *The Huffington Post*, argues "The problem, in a nutshell, is this: The old economic model has utterly failed us. It has destroyed our communities, our democracy, our economic security, and the planet we live on. The old industrial-age systems-- state communism, fascism, free-market capitalism-- have all let us down hard."

A study by Deloitte's *Center for the Edge* shows that the effectiveness of management in organizations has been steadily falling for the last 50 years. Management guru Steve Denning, writing in an article in *Forbes* magazine cites data that shows the life expectancy of firms in the Fortune 500 is now less than 15 years and rapidly declining. He also cites data from the Kaufmann Foundation which indicates between 1980-2005, firms older than 5 years created net zero jobs in the U.S. Denning argues that the economy and world of business today, with the advent of globalization, the Internet, and social media have changed everything, and the result on management-driven hierarchical bureaucracies is devastating. "Now the power in the marketplace has shifted from seller to buyer," Denning contends, "And in this new ecosystem, big lumbering bureaucracies of the 20th century are not agile enough to compete." And yet, management consultants, business schools and governments still don't get it, Denning says.

What's needed is a paradigm shift. "It's really a change in an ecosystem," from a hierarchical bureaucracy that is internally focused on production outputs to an ecosystem that is agile, flexible and externally focused on clients, Denning argues. It's also a change "from a world in which workers and customers are manipulated as things to a world in which workers and customers are interacted with as human beings." It's a shift from a boss/manager centric world to a customer-centered world. Management guru Gary Hamel says, "Management is out of date, like the combustion engine, a technology that has stopped evolving."

Jeffrey Pfeffer and Christina Fong, writing in the *Academy of Management Learning and Education,* argue that research shows business schools have limited influence over management practices in organizations. Harold Leavitt, writing in the *California Management Review,* says cryptically of business schools that they produce "critters with lopsided brains, icy hearts and shrunken souls."

Thomas Hout, writing in the *Harvard Business Review,* argues that if management is so good at predicting outcomes through analytical and scientific methods why have so few public companies performed well? "Companies that are managed the traditional way—by executives developing analytically-driven strategy and shaping the organization to meet the needs of the business as they see them—are obsolete. Management as we have come to know it, is too cumbersome."

Howard Sherman and Ron Schultz argue, in their book, *Open Boundaries,* business structures should be self-organized to be successful, which means managers allow employees to organize as needed, based on customer needs. This conclusion places the role of the manager in a very different light.

So there's considerable research evidence to show that traditional management structures and practices no longer work effectively for modern times, and the nature of leadership training in business schools tends to reinforce these obsolete practices. It's been my experience that 90% of the organizations that I have worked with, particularly in the public sector and government, are still run by large and rigid bureaucracies, where a command-and-control leadership style still rules the day. The 10% of the other organizations that I have had the pleasure of working with have flat bureaucracies and the leaders there are very different in their style and focus. More on leadership style in the chapters to come.

The Toxic and Chaotic Workplace
Coincidental with the dysfunctions of current business models, the workplace is becoming increasingly toxic and chaotic.

Stress And Burnout
A scientific analysis of stress over 25 years between 1983 and 2009 was conducted by Carnegie Mellon University. The data suggests there has been

an increase in stress over that time. Those with the higher stresses were women, people with lower incomes and those with less education. Middle-aged men with college degrees and full times jobs saw an increase in their stress levels was almost 200%.

A report by the Center for Creative Leadership entitled *The Stress of Leadership*, concluded 88% of leaders reported work is primary source of stress and 60% said organizations had failed to provide them tools to manage stress.

A study by the non-profit Families and Work Institute showed that one in three American employees are chronically overworked. Key findings of the report included:

- 54% of American employees have felt overwhelmed at some time in the past month
- 89% of employees agreed that they never seem to have enough time to get everything done on the job
- 44% of those who felt overworked were in contact with work at least once a week outside normal working hours.

According to the U.S. National Institute for Occupational Safety, stress related ailments cost companies $200-$300 billion annually. And 70-90% of employee hospital visits are linked to stress.

Stress brings high health care and turnover costs. In a study by Sunday Azagba and Mesbah Sharaf of the Department of Economics at Concordia University of various organizations, health care expenditures for employees with high levels of stress were 46 % greater than at similar organizations without high levels of stress. The authors of the study found that high job stress is associated with higher utilization of health care services.

In particular, workplace stress has been linked to coronary heart disease in retrospective (observing past patterns) and prospective (predicting future patterns) studies. Then there's the impact on turnover: 52 % of employees report that workplace stress has led them to look for a new job, decline a promotion, or leave a job.

Very little in our present culture teaches us when or how to say "no" to unreasonable job demands and mindless working. Today, the average worker works more hours per week than in 2000 and 37% of the population say they work on their vacation. Approximately 50% of executives said they wouldn't use vacation time because there's too much work to do. Work weeks of 60, 80 and even 100 hours a week are common in major law firms and in many major corporations.

It's been my experience in working with many firms, particularly large ones, that overwork is the norm. In a society where job dedication is praised, workaholism is an invisible addiction. Work is at the core of much of modern life. If you work excessively you can be both praised in the corporate world, and criticized because of a lack of work-life balance.

Workaholism is like a badge of courage for many. Professionals are working harder than ever and the 40-hour work week is a thing of the past. Workaholism is a reflection of our culture's embrace of an extreme ethos. For many professionals, work is the center of their social life and friendships.

Personal connections, once made exclusively through family, friends and civic organizations, are now made in the workplace. In conversations with executives and employees alike in the boardrooms and lunchrooms I have visited, the most common comments I hear are phrases such as "I'm up to my neck in alligators," or "I can't keep up," or "not enough time."

Incivility, Harassment and Bullying in the Workplace

Repeated public opinion polls have voiced the concern of Americans and Canadians over the erosion of civility in government, business, media and social media. The most recent poll by Weber Shandwick, reported that 65% of Americans say the lack of civility is a major problem that has worsened during the financial crisis and recession. What's even more distressing is that nearly 50% of those surveyed said they were withdrawing from the basic tenants of democracy—government and politics—because of incivility and bullying.

In two surveys by the Workplace Bullying Institute (WBI) and Zogby International, where bullying was defined as "repeated mistreatment: sabotage by others that prevented work from getting done, verbal abuse, threatening conduct, intimidation and humiliation," 35% of workers experienced bullying first hand, and 62% of the bullies were men. A Harris Interactive poll conducted in 2011 revealed that 34% of women reported being bullied in the workplace.

Stanley Bing wrote in the early 1990s: "So it is today, where bullying behavior is encouraged and rewarded in range of business enterprises. The style itself is applauded in boardrooms and in business publications like *Business Week, as* 'tough,' 'no nonsense,' 'hard as nails.' When you see these code words, you know you're dealing with the bully boss, thanks to the admiration in which bully management is held in American business and academic gurus who perpetuate the techniques."

According to the National Institute of Occupational Safety and Health and a report entitled *Compensation and Working Conditions* conducted by the University of Virginia , in 1998 alone, 700 homicides occurred in the workplace in the U.S. A *U.S. News and World* Report poll says that 89% of U.S. workers said incivility is a serious problem and 78% said it is getting worse. The cost of workplace violence to employers is estimated somewhere up to $36 billion annually. The major culprits in bullying in the workplace are leaders. Inside Silicon Valley, arrogance runs rampant and investors seem to reward ruthless behavior with piles of cash.

An example of this arrogance and ruthlessness is Mark Zuckerberg. He reportedly stole his business idea from the Winklevoss twins. "Yah, I'm going to f--- them," he told a friend over IM about the pair--"Probably in the ear." Snapchat CEO Evan Spiegel wrote a number of misogynistic-sounding emails when he was in college to his fraternity brothers. Twitter's co-founders back-stabbed each other repeatedly: Founder Noah Glass was booted out of the company. Ev Williams and Jack Dorsey were both given, and then stripped of, the CEO title. Even Steve Jobs, one of the world's most-praised entrepreneurs, was said to have two sides. Jobs' biographer, Walter Isaacson, portrayed the late Apple CEO as "Good Steve" and "Bad Steve." An example: Jobs once stormed into a meeting and called everyone "f---ing dickless a--holes."

Our society rewards leaders who are bullies as long as they produce bottom-line results, which are almost exclusively measured in financial returns to shareholders.

I've personally witnessed the bullying behavior of executives and supervisors in organizations, sometimes overt, and sometimes very subtle, and the effect on employees in the organization is viral-like, and in time it permeates the organization.

Mental Health Issues In The Workplace
Mental health issues are a silent tsunami in the workplace, one that could engulf organizations in myriad of productivity and profitability problems as well as legal liabilities unless mental health is addressed as seriously as are marketing, compensation and strategic plans.

In an article in the *Wall Street Journal*, Melissa Korn contends that "it's becoming problematic for companies as an increasing number of adults seek treatment for psychiatric disorders." According to the U.S. National Institute of Mental Health, more than one in four American adults has a diagnosable mental health disorder, and one in seventeen has a serious disorder such as schizophrenia or bipolar disorder, but chances are co-workers or managers don't know who they are.

According to a *U.S.A. Today* report, based on research by Harvard University Medical School, untreated mental illness costs the U.S. a minimum of $105 billion in lost productivity each year. Most organizations' health coverage plans show that physical ailments are covered, while mental health problems lag far behind.

According to a 2008 study by Mercer, mental illness is estimated to result in 35 million workdays lost each year. The Conference Board of Canada's study, "Building Healthy Workplaces," estimates that 44% of Canadians say they've coped with a mental health problem such as extreme stress, substance abuse, schizophrenia, depression, burnout and addictions. The report went on to state that almost 50% of managers had no training in managing workers with mental health issues.

Martin Shain, in a recent report for the Mental Health Commission of Canada, titled, "The Road to Psychological Safety: Legal, Scientific and Social Foundations for a national Standard for Psychological Safety," argues that "normal" resilient people can be brought to the brink of mental distress and sometimes pushed over the edge by conditions at work. Mental ill-health, Shain argues, can result in psychologically unsafe workplaces, possibly in the form of debilitating anxiety, depression, and burnout or even cardiovascular disease, higher consumption of alcohol and susceptibility to infectious diseases. Mental health problems can occur also when job demands and requirements exceed worker skill levels, and when employees don't have control over the means, manner and methods of their work.

Shain's 2010 update report states, "a political legal storm is brewing in the area of mental health protection at work. This storm brings with it a rising tide of liability for employers." He points out those financial rewards for damages against employers have increased by as much as 700% in the past five years.

One difficulty that employees or potential hires who are suffering from mental health issues face is declaring their condition openly. Many recruiters will tell you, although not always on the record, that an admission of mental health issues raises "red flags," and can be a factor in employer decision-making.

I was brought in to facilitate teamwork in a group of professionals who were experiencing high levels of conflict and stress. After individual interviews with the team members and attending and observing several of their meetings, it became apparent that trust, mutual respect and appropriate communication and engagement skills were lacking.

But even more pronounced was the fact that one particular team member was suffering from severe psychological stress as a result of personal issues, and he brought that stress with him to the meetings. While there was recognition by the team members and the team leader of his difficulties, no efforts had been made to address this issue by the team or the organization as a whole. And while his behavior was disruptive at times, the team's ability to cooperatively work together, practice appropriate emotional intelligence and emotional regulation was not well developed.

Productivity And Employee Engagement Problems
Employee engagement levels and productivity have been consistently declining in the last decade, according to studies by the Gallup organization, the Hay Group and other research studies.

The subject of employee engagement as a measure of productivity and management strategies to increase engagement has been a hot topic since the original Gallup organization research was published. While most of the research identifies low levels of employee engagement in many organizations and strategies to increase that engagement for the purpose of improving productivity, the cause-and-effect relationship is not overwhelming. Rather, an overarching strategy of increasing employee well-being in which engagement strategies are incorporated, appears to be more favorable.

The Gallup organization defined employee engagement as "an employee's involvement with, commitment to, and satisfaction with work." Research conducted in the past decade has shown that employee engagement has declined significantly in most industries, with some research citing as few as 29% of employees being actively engaged in their jobs. The Hay Group found in its research that among office workers who were actively engaged, they were 43% more productive.

In a study for the American Psychological Association, researchers James Harter, Frank Schmidt and Corey Keyes concluded in a report entitled, *Well-Being in the Workplace and its Relationship to Business Outcomes*, productivity was enhanced in workplaces where daily occurrences that bring about joy, interest, and caring lead to high level of bonding of individuals to each other, their work and their organization. The authors concluded that well-being in the workplace is, in part, a function of helping employees do what is naturally right for them by freeing them to do so--through behaviors that influence employee engagement and therefore that increase the frequency of positive emotions.

Traditional Responses To Workplace Problems

Each year, HR Departments are faced with a variety of employee problems that detract from the corporate bottom line. Topping the list are workplace stress and anxiety, which contribute to a host of other issues, including chronic illness and absenteeism, dissatisfaction and burnout, inattention and inefficiency, reduced creativity and workplace conflict.

In their attempts to deal with these problems, businesses have implemented a host of measures, some very expensive, including:

- Employee manuals
- Stress management programs
- Psychological counseling
- EAP programs
- Organizational restructuring
- Team building retreats
- Health education

But despite these attempts, the problems stubbornly exist, particularly stress, workplace conflict, and anxiety.

Companies around the world spend up to $100 billion a year to train employees in the skills they need to improve corporate performance—topics such as communication, sales techniques, performance management, or lean operations. But training typically doesn't have much impact. Indeed, only 25% of the respondents to a recent McKinsey survey said their training programs measurably improved business performance, and most companies don't even bother to track the returns they get on their investments in training.

Signs Of A Toxic And Unproductive Workplace:

1. All sticks and no carrots. Management focuses solely on what employees are doing wrong or correcting problems, and rarely give positive feedback for what is going right.

2. The creeping bureaucracy. There are too many levels of approval and management to get things done.
3. The gigantic bottom line. A singular focus on profits, beating the competition and cost cutting without consideration of other bottom lines.
4. When bullies rule the roost. Bullying of employees by management, or tolerated by management when it occurs among employees.
5. Losing the human touch. People are considered to be objects, with little concern for their happiness and/or well-being.
6. High levels of stress, turnover, absenteeism and burnout.
7. Rampant multitasking by employees and managers.
8. A focus on "fixing" employees instead of structuring healthy workplaces.

As an executive coach, working in small, medium sized and large organizations, I've observed that the issue of employee engagement is not a simple matter of measuring employee at task productivity. While most of the research identifies low levels of employee engagement and subsequent strategies in a cause-and-effect manner, the evidence is not overwhelming. I believe, and have seen that an overarching strategy of increasing employee well-being in which engagement strategies are incorporated, is more favorable.

Engagement strategies need to be replaced with human capital strategies by determining what are the human drivers of business results, and which drivers can actually be shown to improve human performance. My experience is reflected in a study for the American Psychological Association, researchers James Harter, Frank Schmidt and Corey Keyes who concluded in a report entitled, *Well-Being in the Workplace and its Relationship to Business Outcomes,* productivity was enhanced in workplaces where daily occurrences that bring about joy, interest, and caring that lead to high levels of bonding of individuals to each other, their work, and their organization, was the most effective.

And one of the measures that matters most is the frequency of positive emotions. Our workplaces are less desirable than they should be in terms of employee well-being and productivity. The result is a workplace in a continual chaotic storm of turbulence. Traditional methods of training and assistance have had a moderate positive impact on toxic and turbulent workplaces.

The state of employees' mind and emotions or their internal life has been given little or no attention. We need to turn our mindless workplaces into mindful workplaces. We need to seek out the eye in the storm.

Summary of Key Points:

- The current paradigm of organizations, based on free market capitalism which focuses on short term profits and shareholder value, has created dysfunctional workplaces and damaged our economic and environment well-being
- Stress in the workplace has reached epidemic proportions affecting employee well-being, employer healthcare costs and productivity
- Incidents of workplace bullying, harassment and conflict are on the rise
- Mental health issues are the silent Tsunami affecting workplace culture and productivity
- Traditional approaches to address toxic workplace issues have had limited success
- The structure of corporations, management structures and excessive focus on the financial bottom line have had a detrimental impact on employee well-being
- Mindlessness in the workplace, often created by multitasking and lack of focus, is unappreciated
- Traditional strategies to address these issues have had only low to moderate success.

To get more detailed resources on the Toxic Corporation and the Toxic Workplace, go to my website at http://raywilliams.ca

2 MINDLESSNESS AT WORK

Mindlessness at work has become a global touchstone of mockery, and entertainers have enchanted audiences worldwide with comedies featuring mindless managers. In the TV series "The Office," Steve Carrell, playing the role of Michael Scott as Regional Manager of a Dunder-Mifflin branch in Scranton, Pennsylvania, epitomizes mindless behavior, which is characterized by a reliance on old, often outdated categories and a reduced awareness of one's social and physical world. While some argue that mindlessness is a necessity in the work environment, a closer examination reveals that mindlessness is rarely, if ever, beneficial because it closes us off to creative possibilities, freezes our responses, and prevents needed change.

Mindlessness can be part of the cultural makeup of an organization. The movie "Office Space" highlights the mindless business culture many people experience as employees. In such a workplace, categories of thinking are rarely revisited, context rarely matters, and individual differences and strengths are irrelevant to the job. The character Milton in the movie exemplifies such a mindless bureaucrat, who can only function in a culture that values mindless behavior. The main character, Peter, ultimately gets fed up by this mindless culture after several bosses ask him whether he had read an irrelevant office memo. This story highlights how a culture of mindlessness can lead employees to unhappiness and active disengagement. Active disengagement occurs when employees start undermining the company by sabotaging its operations. Peter and two of his co-workers in the film take revenge by developing a plot to tweak the payment system so that small sums of customer payments will be transferred to their account.

Mindless individuals are much like robots--thoughts, emotions, and behaviors-- are determined by programmed routines based on things learned in the past. It is theorized that mindlessness is often a consequence of the tendency to apply previously formed mindsets to current situations, which lock individuals into a repetitive and often unconscious approach to daily life.

Mindless working is this century's cocaine, a problem with no name.

Cognitive Overload

The average American consumes 34 gigabytes of content and 100,000 words every single day, according to the 2008 report from University of California, San Diego. To put these numbers in perspective, one gigabyte is a symphony in high-fidelity sound or a broadcast quality movie.

Our colossal consuming habits are not only crowding out essential neurological downtime, but they're creating a chemical addiction. When we consume media -- from watching TV to surfing the Net, and from playing videogames to using social media -- we're triggering the brain chemical dopamine. Dopamine creates a "high," and we are wired to do what it takes to maintain this elevated state. When the dopamine levels decrease, we begin to look for diversions that will restore the high.

In the absence of stimulation, and the corresponding dopamine high, we're likely to feel bored. As a result, many of us become stimulation junkies and incessant multitaskers. In the *New York Times* article, "Attached to Technology and Paying the Price," Matt Richtel wrote, "While many people say multitasking makes them more productive, research shows otherwise. Heavy multitaskers actually have more trouble focusing and shutting out irrelevant information, scientists say, and they experience more stress. And scientists are discovering that even after the multitasking ends, fractured thinking and lack of focus persist."

A study of 2,250 adults by two Harvard University psychologists found that peoples' minds wander an astounding 47% of the time. They concluded that a "human mind is a wandering mind, and a wandering mind is a unhappy mind."

Our minds naturally wander. We wander into regrets about the past and worries about the future. We replay scenarios over and over again, not because we want to, but because we can't seem to stop. Wandering minds also compromise the quality of peoples' work. "High quality attention is the productive basis for knowledge workers and we do very little to cultivate that essential resource," says Jeremy Hunter a professor at the Peter F.

Drucker School of Management in Los Angeles.

Mindless workers are disconnected from themselves and see work as a haven for an emotionally unpredictable world; they are on automatic pilot, allowing work to engulf them; they seek an emotional and neurophysiological payoff from frantic working; get an adrenaline rush from meeting impossible deadlines; and they are preoccupied with work no matter where they are.

Teresa Amabie and her colleagues at Harvard Business School evaluated the daily work patterns of more than 9,000 individuals working on projects that required creativity and innovation. They found that the likelihood of creative thinking is higher when people focused on one activity for a significant part of the day and collaborate with only one person. Conversely, when people had fragmented days with many activities and meetings and discussions with lots of people, their creative thinking declined significantly.

CEOs and senior executives calendars are often booked back to back all day based on the proposition that it is both necessary and leads to greater productivity, despite the evidence that it doesn't. CEOs have to learn how to delegate most matters to subordinates, and return contacts from others when convenient. They need to edit or shut off the flow of incoming information and completely unplug for blocks of time, and give up the need to be on top of everything.

Research on multitasking, which often incorrectly, is associated with greater productivity and shows each additional task you undertake concurrently with others reduces performance in them all and it can take up to 15 minutes to restore concentration following a distraction due to a "resetting" process in the brain.

While the brain's basal ganglia operates by distributed association and can draw on almost unlimited capacity, the prefrontal cortex operates via serial processing, has limited daily capacity, and struggles constantly with what to prioritize and bring to conscious thought.

Requiring a serial processor to multitask is a tall order. Studies of multitaskers show that performance deteriorates significantly as soon as they attempt more than one cognitive task at a time. Even though we can comfortably undertake several programmed tasks simultaneously, this is not true of tasks requiring conscious thinking. Try reading an article while watching the news, or adding a list of numbers while someone is speaking to you. Comprehension and retention on both tasks will be compromised. Recent studies into multitasking specifically show deficits in memory and learning when juggling cognitive load.

Research at Duke University underscores why. Researchers found that more than 40 % of our actions are based on habits, not conscious decisions. Unconscious habits and assumptions aren't written in stone, but if we don't bring them into focus then the force of these habits will continue to chart our course.

When negative external events occur, internally the mind ruminates and anxiety and stress increase. We become hijacked by internal suffering. When we practice mindful working, we use our minds to navigate workplace woes with clarity, self-compassion, courage and creativity.

Much of contemporary management and leadership literature emphasizes mere tinkering with a paradigm established in the 19th and 20th centuries. The focus of much of the literature has been on planning, analysis, problem solving and a singular focus on results, with little attention being made to the internal world of leaders—their thoughts and emotions. In this paradigm leaders run on autopilot and can be "mindless."

There's a price to pay for our breakneck speed to continuously improve, and produce. Professors Cyril Bouquet and Ben Bryant, cite in *Forbes* magazine the disastrous collision of two Boeing 747's in the Canary Islands in 1977, killing 583 people, as a case of poor attention management. They argue that two kinds of attention disorders exacerbate the difficulties companies face in economic downturns--fixation and relaxation. In the case of fixation, leaders can be too preoccupied with a few central signals or information; they ignore everything else. With respect to relaxation, Bouquet and Bryant contend that excessive relaxation follows sustained periods of high concentration. They argue that mindfulness can lessen the attention problems of fixation and relaxation.

The demands of leadership can produce what is known as "power stress," a side effect of being in a position of power and influence that often leaves even the best leaders physically and emotionally drained. As a result, leaders can easily find themselves moving from an "approach" orientation to their work characterized by being emotionally open, engaged and innovative, to an "avoidance" orientation that is characterized by aversion, irritability, aggression, fear and close-mindedness.

If leaders believe they don't have the time to work through all aspects of a problem they are inclined to be narrow in perspective and take cognitive shortcuts, and become more impulsive and reactive. Their actions, in effect become "mindless" and automatic.

Daniel Siegel, a neuroscientist and author of *The Mindful Brain: Reflection and Attunement in the Cultivation of Well-Being*, contends that a corporate culture of cognitive shortcuts results in oversimplication, curtailed curiosity, reliance on ingrained beliefs and the development of perceptional blind spots. He argues that mindfulness practices enable individuals to jettison judgment and develop more flexible feelings toward what before may have been mental events they tried to avoid, or towards which they had intense averse reactions.

David Rock, writing in *Psychology Today*, argues "busy people who run our companies and institutions tend to spend little time thinking about themselves and other people, but a lot of time thinking about strategy, data and systems. As a result the circuits involved in thinking about oneself and other people, the medial prefrontal cortex, tends to be not too well developed." Rock says "speaking to an executive about mindfulness can be a bit like speaking to a classical musician about jazz."

I can relate two stories here from my experience in working with senior executives. The first involves a large non-profit organization in which the CEO had been with the organization for two decades. When I was engaged by the organization, it was having financial difficulties due to declining a declining membership and declining revenues from other sources. Services and programs to members had not substantially changed for over a decade, it was apparent the organization was not keeping up with the times. In meeting with employees and leaders in the organization, I was struck with how limiting discussions were regarding planning for change. Rarely were new ideas presented, or discussed fully when they were presented.

Rather, discussions and plans revolved around the assumption that things would be done the way they always were done, expecting that results would be different. The meetings and discussions had a "mindless" quality to them, where memories of things past drove decisions, and an automatic agreement with things "the way they are," pervaded relationships. In that kind of culture, new ideas were not incubated.

The second example was an organization where the leader was a command-and-control leader, of long standing whom employees feared. Rarely did employees have the courage to suggest new ideas or to provide critical feedback on the way things were being done, even though the organization was experiencing difficult times competing with a more progressive organization. The leader of the organization considered any constructive feedback or new ideas to be questioning his authority and he reacted aggressively. He often would respond to challenges by reminding people how successful he had been in the past, and that all his ideas had always worked. Again, a mindlessness had crept into the leader's behavior and infected employees in the organization.

There's an irony here. The very structures and systems created by the industrial era and the corporate paradigm, with their focus on set procedures, rules, manuals and automated human behavior are the very things that contribute to people in organizations acting in a mindless, "autopilot" way, often devoid of creativity, passion, joy and happiness—and eventually at the expense of productivity.

Summary of Key Points:

- The modern organization with its roots in the industrial era with systems of rules, regulations and standardized processes has contributed to workers and leaders who run on "autopilot" or mindlessly
- The prevalence of multitasking can contribute to mindlessness
- Mindlessness can be traced to fixed mindsets, and rigid assumptions about the way things should be
- Creative and innovate processes and outcomes require using the parts of our brains that are reflective, curious, and open minded, antithetical to mindlessness.

To get more detailed resources on the nature of mindlessness and what to do about it, go to my website at: http://raywilliams.ca

3 THE COMING REVOLUTION IN THE WAY WE WORK

We are now experiencing huge structural changes in our economic and social lives, which will forever change the world of work. And the acceleration of these changes will be constant and unrelenting. Power is shifting slowly but assuredly to individuals who will have real time 24/7 access to tools and information previously afforded only to those in power.

The advent of personal technology for workers and consumers will give them new power. We will see increasingly an alignment between the characteristics and needs of consumers and workers. Shifting demographics, particularly the younger generations will drive this shift.

The new consumers are always connected; share their opinions; have an abundance of choice; requires immediacy; seek authenticity; and value responsibility. What will emerge in 2015 is a new employee who increasingly reflects those characteristics of the new consumer, especially with the increasing shifting demographics in the workforce. Younger generations like Millennials and Generation Z will make their workforce entrances, and they will bring different needs and expectations to work. We will also see an increase in contingent workers who will change how work is done.

What's Happening To Jobs?
Mike Dorning, in his article in *Bloomberg Businessweek* cites U.S. employment data that is frightening. The portion of all men holding any kind of job in the U.S. is 63.5%, the lowest figure since 1948. In comparison, in 1969, 95% of men in the prime working years had a job. The temporary placement company in the U.S., Adecco, predicts that the rate of growth in contingent workers will be three to four times the growth rate of traditional jobs and will soon comprise at least 30% or more of the global workforce. Douglas Rushkoff, author of *Life Inc: How the World Became a Corporation and*

How To Take It Back, was interviewed by CNN.com. He proposed the notion that jobs are obsolete. He argues that it's not a bad thing that technology is replacing jobs. Part of the public discourse has focused on employment as the solution to economic growth, but countries have in fact focused on productivity through technology, not human labor, Rushkoff contends. The U.S. and Canada are productive enough to provide everyone sufficient shelter, food, education and health care without increased employment. The problem is the proceeds of productivity -- economic wealth -- are not equitably distributed. The U.N. Food and Agriculture Organization reports that there is enough food produced in the world to provide the entire world's population with 2,720 calories per day. Yet every six seconds a child dies from malnutrition.

So is the problem that we don't have enough "stuff" for everyone or that we don't have enough ways for people to work and prove they deserve the stuff? And why do some people need obscene amounts of stuff?

Let's remember that the concept of jobs is a relatively new idea. People may have always worked, but until the advent of corporate business in the Renaissance, most people worked for themselves. The advent of the Industrial Age made most jobs as menial and unskilled as possible. As technology in factories was used to increase production and use less labor, so too has digital technology supplanted jobs. One of the biggest problems we face today is how to create full employment while pursuing technology that is intended to replace it.

Sara Horowitz, founder and CEO of Freelancers Union, argues that the jobless future is already here. She points out that many people are already combining part-time work just to get by. In an article in *Atlantic* magazine, Horowitz says that as of 2005, a full 30% of the workforce has participated in this "freelance economy," and entrepreneurial activity reached an all time high in 2010. Dana Shaw, former senior Vice-President for Staffing Industry Analysts, reported that in the Fortune 100 companies, contingent workers make up 20-30% of the workforce, but predicts it will soon be 50%. Statistics Canada reported that by 2009, 52% of all temporary jobs were contract jobs, 25% of them were professional. The permanent full time jobs that were jettisoned during the recession are not likely to return.

McKinsey &Co. reported that 65% of U.S. corporations have restructured their workforce and have no plans to return to pre-recession employment, but rather are opting for contingent and contract work when the need for expansion takes place.

Marshall Brain, writing in his informative blog, cites the explosive growth in the use of robotics - not only on the assembly line but also in ordinary retail businesses, including McDonalds, Home Depot, and others. Brain cites the principle of Moore's Law – that CPU power in microprocessor chips doubles every 18 to 24 months – to support his argument that a massive number of jobs will be replaced by technology and never return. He forecasts that almost all construction, manufacturing, transportation, wholesale, retail, and hotel and restaurant jobs will be lost to automation by the year 2050. This would create unemployment levels of up to 50%.

Besides the negative impact of increased unemployment, the expansion of temporary work has other downsides. One of the biggest hurdles that will have to be overcome for contingent work is the predominant attitude in organizations that contract workers are less important or less competent, and less committed than "permanent" workers. Contingent work also is accompanied by a lack of benefits such as health, life and disability insurance. Some experts would argue that the growth of contingent and contract jobs contributes to the growing problem of income gap between the wealthy and the rest of society, as contract workers tend to be paid less and earn less than permanent workers. People who don't earn as much money or have less economic security tend to spend less as consumers, which has a general negative impact on the economy. A second argument, which is reflected in an OECD report, is that contingent and part-time work produces more stress for these workers, who may be continually fearful of loss of employment. This in turn, has potential health cost implications for the organizations.

Many economists argue that the current economic problem is lack of consumer demand—the lack of money to spend on stuff. But with the increasing decline of the middle class who spends most of that money, the problem won't be solved any time soon. So while politicians and business leaders chant for more jobs, the real issue is economic inequality to support sustained growth. It's not likely that the 45 million plus people at the poverty level in the U.S. will drive its economy to new prosperity. A documentary film "Humans Need Not Apply," shows that with more tasks being done by machines, a full 45% of the current workforce can be replaced by technology that is available today.

From burger bots that can make a hamburger every ten seconds to machines that perform scientific experiments and write their own code, automated devices are finding their way into virtually every area of human endeavor. No matter what degree a student pursues today, its ability to provide employment to its holder cannot no longer be guaranteed.

Employee Engagement Levels Are Declining
Just 30 % of employees in America feel engaged at work, according to a 2013 report by Gallup, which means 70% are not engaged. Around the world, across 142 countries, the proportion of employees who feel engaged at work is just 13 %. For most of us, in short, work is a depleting, dispiriting experience, and in some obvious ways, it's getting worse. Demand for our time is increasingly exceeding our capacity — draining us of the energy we need to bring our skill and talent fully to life. Increased competitiveness and a leaner, post-recession work force add to the pressures. The rise of digital technology is perhaps the biggest influence, exposing us to an unprecedented flood of information and requests that we feel compelled to read and respond to at all hours of the day and night.

A 2012 global work force study of 32,000 employees by the consulting company Towers Watson found that the traditional definition of engagement — the willingness of employees to voluntarily expend extra effort — is no longer sufficient to fuel the highest levels of performance. Willing, it turns out, does not guarantee able. Companies in the Towers Watson study with high engagement scores measured in the traditional way had an operating margin of 14 %. By contrast, companies with the highest number of "sustainably engaged" employees had an operating margin of 27 %, nearly three times those with the lowest traditional engagement scores.

What The New Workplace And Work Will Look Like
Until recently jobs defined us as members of a structured society moving toward unified goals. "Probably no other sentence comes up at a party as often as: 'So, what do you do?,'" the Berlin critic Patrick Spaet wrote in the *Baffler*, "There is an unspoken question behind this: 'Are you useful? Work determines our social status: tell me what your job is—and I'll tell you who you are." The work fetish has become deeply ingrained in the DNA of western industrial nations, Spaet continues. And why should it not?

The job has been our friend, a contract between an individual and a larger group thereof that they will not be left behind so long as they continue to fulfill their duties. But our commitment to the job has wavered, and our fetish for work is wavering as the nature of labor and who benefits from it has changed.

A report, *The Future of Work*, by U.S. consulting firm, PSFK Labs, one of the most interesting of the reports, contained these conclusions and predictions about the future of work:

- **On demand staffing**: an algorithm against the company's changing needs will match the skills and availability of employees and freelance contractors. This implies the disappearance of a large permanent workforce
- **Collision collusion**: Physical, mobile and web workspaces will be designed to ensure critical interaction among colleagues, vendors, partners and customers
- **Improvised workplace**: With a flick of the switch, furniture and software will adapt to the changing needs of the organization. This will include pop-up or temporary workplaces
- **Living Knowledge**: Information will flow across and up-and-down the organization constantly; instantly accessible by anyone who wants it. Networked knowledge and social workflow are the keys here
- **Constant Learning**: Employee empowered education will help them own the direction of the company. This includes more learning by doing and employees as equal stakeholders to shareholders. This may help to revolutionize formal education institutions as well.

Ariel Schwartz, writing in the blog, *Co-Exist*, describes the PSFK vision well. PSFK imagines that learning initiatives for young entrepreneurs, such as Enstitute, will become the norm. In this model, college students are matched up with startups, where they learn all the programs used by the company, take relevant Skillshare classes, and work on projects, and sit in on panels. Virtual learning libraries, where entrepreneurial experts can leave advice in written and video form, will also proliferate (we're seeing hints of this now with the growing online education industry). At the same time, skills marketplaces--social tools that allow employers to quickly get a handle on applicants' skills-- will become popular. Mozilla's Open Project, for example, lets people display their skills via badges on social media profiles.

A PWC report on the future of work provided these insights:

- With the aid of technology, assembly workers will wear devices that gauge their concentration, work rate, moods and physical energy levels
- The higher education system as it is now structured will be transformed because of unsustainable costs and limited job opportunities for graduates
- Managing complexity and ambiguity will have the single biggest

impact on the way we work

- Social responsibility will dominate the corporate agenda with prime concerns about the environment and peoples' well-being
- Companies will break down into collaboration networks of smaller organizations
- Work in one profession or a job for an extended period of time will disappear
- Leadership teams will replace single leaders, with their prime focus on developing positive and inclusive corporate cultures
- The Internet of Things will shape our economy and the way we work
- The social contract will be revised with an emphasis on ethical values and work-life balance
- Work will be restructured on the basis of flexibility, employee autonomy and career challenges/opportunities in return for short-term or contractual employment
- Workers will increasingly see themselves as members of a particular skill (e.g., guild) or professional network rather than as an employee of a particular company
- Workers will be rewarded based on their expertise and results rather than position and length of service, and therefore will have an increasing personal stake in the success of work
- Learning and training will become flexible, personalized and collaborative.

Josh Bersin, President and CEO of Bersin & Associates, a talent management company, wrote a insightful article on the issue, arguing, "jobs are turning into roles, roles are becoming more specialized and the new currency of value is expertise, not simply experience." Our traditional vision of a job is history. It was a functional role defined by a set of skills, or competencies that carried out a specific function, and along with it came a title and career path that was clearly defined. Job descriptions were written and people were hired to them and the HR function was created to manage the process.

Bersin has coined the term "the borderless workplace," which means workers work seamlessly inside and outside organizations, adapting to change in world conditions. Penelope Trunk, writing in her popular blog on the workplace, contends that we will see the end of what we conceive of as "office life," within a short time and that employers will increasingly view all their employees as "consultants" to facilitate flexible hours and project based work; and we will see the end of the traditional career path and organizational hierarchies.

How Generation Y Will Change The Workplace

By 2025, between 50-75 % of the world's employees will be young people (ie., the Millennial Generation or Gen Y). The prospects for economic prosperity for this generation are not particularly encouraging, and yet Millennials have high and positive expectations.

Millennials are optimistic and connected. According to Erica Dhawan, a former MBA student at MIT and MPA at Harvard, specializing in Gen Y, and a featured speaker at the World Economic Forum at Davos, Switzerland: "Technology has convinced Millennials that a single person's voice can make a difference." She goes on to argue that Millennials want to be coached, not supervised and mentored formally by older generations. Josh Bersin, writing in *Forbes* about Millennials cites a study by Deloitte and a similar study in India which shows nearly 50 % of the Millennials in the studies are already in leadership positions, and "most companies are discovering that supporting and retaining this talent requires a new way of doing business."

Kate Taylor, writing in *Forbes*, states, "The nine to five job may soon be a relic of the past if Millennials have their way...Freelancing and self-employment are on the rise. Meanwhile 60% of Millennials are leaving their companies in less than three years at a cost to the organization of $20,000 per person to replace."

According to Dan Schawbel, author of *Promote Yourself: The New Rules for Career Success* and an expert on the Millennials, says "Millennials have a different view of how work should be done and what a company's role should be in society. They want companies to give back to the community; to eliminate the traditional nine to five workday; collaboration instead of isolation; and to create a organization fabricated by social media. Millennials, relative to older generations, are all about giving back to communities that align with their core values.

Some key findings Deloitte's third annual Millennial Survey of nearly 7,800 Millennials from 28 countries across Western Europe, North America, Latin America, BRICS, and Asia-Pacific about business, government, and innovation are:

- While most Millennials believe business is having a positive impact on society and increasing prosperity, they think business can do much more to address society's challenges in the areas of most concern: resource scarcity, climate change, and income inequality

- 80 % of Millennials surveyed want to work for a business with ethical practices
- Millennials say government has the greatest potential to address society's biggest issues but it is failing to do so
- Millennials believe the biggest barrier to innovation is management's attitude
- Millennials believe the success of a business should be measured in terms of more than just its financial performance, with a focus on improving society among the most important things it should seek to achieve
- Millennials are also charitable and keen to participate in "public life"; donate to charities; actively volunteer; and be members of a community organization.

These reports underscore a number of Millennial studies in recent years, with particular reference to Millennials' different attitudes and expectations towards work and careers compared to the current dominant Baby Boomers. Also clear is Millennials' definition of loyalty to the organization and expectations for frequent career or job changes. Millennials have a very different perspective and expectation of the role and behavior of managers, seeing them more in an encouraging, coaching, and peer capacity, something that is currently at odds with the current generation of Baby Boomer managers who see their role as one associated more with power and position.

It's becoming clear through these reports and the current socio-demographic changes occurring that both businesses and governments will need to pay a lot more attention to structuring the workplace and social policy to better adapt to the realities of the next generation. The Millennial generation or Gen Y is transforming the nature of careers and the workplace. Their values, beliefs and life style are significantly different from the Baby Boomer generation. These differences will require organizations to adapt due to sheer numbers of Millennials who will dominate the workplace in the coming decade.

I've had the privilege of working with scores of young Millennials in chairing the Vancouver Board of Trade's *Leaders of Tomorrow* mentoring program, and personally being a mentor with them. I've found these young people to be passionate and driven to make a difference in the world, and confident they can assume the role of leaders early in their careers. And clearly they see their careers and the workplace very differently than current Baby Boomers.

While they may at times be impatient and overconfident, they desperately want to be coached and mentored, and have incredible leadership skills to offer at a young age. The entrenched Baby Boomers who have dominated our systems to date are missing the boat to not take advantage of what Millennials have to offer—now!

Workers today are becoming more entrepreneurial and mobile, which makes many bureaucratic organizations less appealing to them. Even though there have been numerous management experiments with "flatter" organizations and a multitude of worker benefits, most organizations are still structured according to an outmoded paradigm of work, where efficiency and conformity rule.

Mario Kaphan and his colleagues at the Brazilian e-recruiting company Vagas.com have a singular design for a radically open, free, and entrepreneurial organization. Kaphan describes the company's 15-year experiment in managing without managers. Vagas.com has no hierarchy, no titles, and no formal rules. Individual "members" enjoy a remarkable degree of autonomy and collegiality (the mantra is "individuals are empowered to do whatever they want but everybody has everything to do with that"). All work is done in small, self-managed teams, and decisions are made via reasoned debate and consensus — an initially laborious process that all members practice daily and that yields powerful results.

At Vagas, every management process — from performance reviews and rewards to strategy — is highly participative. Rather than rigid planning and budget cycles, the rhythm of the organization is set on a rolling two-week management cycle — each team meets fortnightly to review progress. The result is a fast-growing, entrepreneurial organization.

Another example is Wellington, New Zealand-based Enspiral, a path-breaking collective of professionals and social enterprises driven by the desire to change the world. As an entirely new kind of organization — a collective of individuals with a common ideal working on different problems with radically distributed resources, information, and control — the Enspiral team found itself tackling and disrupting just about every core management process, from decision-making and direction setting to budgeting. Another example is Andrew Jones' Nomatik Coworking hack which aims to build community and connection beyond the walls of any particular organization.

Nomatik is a clever social platform designed to extend the spirit of co-working beyond actual co-working spaces, to engineer productive matches between individual talents and organizations, and to reimagine the boundaries of the organization in the process.

Jones' approach acknowledges that no single organization will ever be able to directly employ all of the relevant, talented people who could make valuable contributions. And, just as important, colleagues aren't necessarily the people who sit next to you at work, but rather the people who are working on the same problems with the same passion that you have.

The organizations and leaders who figure out the most clever and compelling ways to connect those people and organizations will be the real winners in the creative economy.

The Greyston Bakery in Yonkers, New York, hires, trains, and houses people who are facing difficult life circumstances. Greyston even supplies brownies to Ben and Jerry's ice cream factory in Vermont. The company's motto: "We don't hire people to bake brownies; we bake brownies to hire people."

In Easthampton, Massachusetts, Prosperity Candle trains recent immigrants how to make candles, and keeps them on as employees. They go from being on welfare, to supporting themselves and their families. And that's the point, says Prosperity's founder, Ted Barber, "We are a for-profit company with the heart of a non-profit."

"B Corporations" have a double bottom line; they benefit society while making a profit. This double mission alerts shareholders that they will pursue their social mission even if it means a lull in return on investment. For example, Patagonia, the American maker of sports clothing, has long been a B corporation. This allowed them to conduct years of research to invent a rubber derived from a desert shrub, not petroleum, to use in their products. Buy your eyeglass frames from Warby Parker. They give a pair of glasses to a person in the developing world for every frame they sell. These companies recreate business models to be meaningful, not just profitable.

Grameen Bank in Bangladesh was one of the first to adopt this approach by giving micro-loans to help people in poverty start their own small businesses. The rate of repayment has been so high that they have been able to re-loan the funds over and over, creating thousands of entrepreneurial small businesses.

Other organizations are shifting their business-as-usual missions to include a more conscious capitalism approach. As part of a larger sustainability goal,

Unilever plans to give technical aid to small farmers in developing nations so they can join the company's supply chain as dependable sources. Huge companies like Unilever can take a social mission to scale. Unilever's goal is 500,000 small farms.

The psychological contract between employers and employees is shifting. While receiving a steady paycheck is still an integral component of employment there is growing desire for work to be fulfilling on a relationship level that extends beyond financial compensation. In today's workplace loyalty is just as likely to mean being true to oneself, as it is to mean being loyal to one's firm.

The Need For Mindful Workplaces
The financial protection specialist company Unum, partnering with The Future Laboratory, has released a report, entitled *The Future Workplace: Key Trends That Will Affect Employee Well-being and How to Prepare for Them Today.* The report examines in detail how the workplace is evolving and what employers need to do to manage employee well-being in the next 15 years. The study was based on a survey of 1,000 British workers and insights from a group of leading experts from the Futures 100 Network. The report identifies four major forces or trends that will deeply impact the workplace, and for which employers need to develop action strategies:

- **Ageless:** A workplace which allows "returnment," or encouraging older workers to remain or return to the workplace instead of retiring, and sees workers energized to continue to work until a later age because they want to, rather than have to
- **Mindful:** A workplace which nurtures mental health and encourages workers to recharge mentally and achieve balance in their busy hyper-connected, digital lifestyles
- **Intuitive:** A workplace that uses data and insight on its workers' environment, mood, wants and needs to create an all-encompassing, intelligent and intuitive environment
- **Collaborative:** A workplace that embraces the collapse of traditional structures to promote open and social exchange, operating a flat structure and embracing the impact of more women in the workplace.

Recognizing the importance of the mindfulness trend, the report concludes, "employers must integrate mindfulness throughout their businesses, from the way employees talk to each other and conduct meetings to the way success is measured, projects are managed and people are rewarded. Being mindful is about standing back and reflecting on what a company does and how that affects everything around it."

The report emphasizes the importance of downtime as a way not only of addressing well-being, but also productivity, a conclusion supported by several recent studies. In a surprising perspective, the value of daydreaming was emphasized: "Employees and employers should realize the power of daydreaming and give people the time space and tools to imagine more. Organizations will generate more ideas, solutions and profits if they embrace the art of daydreaming. Employers who shut out daydreaming and creativity will suffer financially, because ultimately clients and customers will see an organization that doesn't think before it acts."

The report concludes that what is needed is "the rise of a workplace that is mindful, tranquil, sublime and that nurtures the health and performance of the mind." This conclusion was based on the observation that workers are "turning away from their busy, hyper-connected, digital lifestyles and prioritizing personal fulfillment and well-being instead". Workplace care in 2030 will need to deliver a new set of values. Instead of being "always on," there will be digital invisibility; instead of conversation, there will be contemplation; and there will be quiet sublime spaces within buildings and within organizations.

Mindful workers are feeling overwhelmed by the tools and means of communication they have to use on a daily basis, the report concludes. Employers need to stress the importance of regular breaks to improve productivity and allow employees to relax their minds for a while. In a clear change of direction, employers also need to establish an organizational culture in which overwork and workaholism are not only unappreciated, but there should be company policies that prohibit it. Also, employees have consistently indicated, in numerous surveys, that they want greater control over their work time and personal time and would prefer to work in an environment that supports flexible working and mixing of teams, rather than a set structure.

Peter O'Donnell, CEO of Unum argues "The workplace is changing, becoming increasingly people-centric, so organizations competing for talent will need to be more supportive of their staff than ever before. Employers need to start taking steps now to adapt effectively to its evolution or they face significant financial repercussions."

Tom Savigar, Chief Strategy Officer at The Future Laboratory and co-author of the report says, "An ageless and mindful workplace is what British workers truly want to see their employers embracing so there is a clear need for businesses to augment how they care for the mind as well as the body to enable their staff to work better and for longer." In advocating a more collaborative workplace, the report boldly states, "In an increasingly social, transparent and interdependent world, the traits that are traditionally considered to be masculine—decisiveness, aggression, resilience, pride and analytical skills—will no longer be effective."

An additional insightful note in the report addresses the issue of gender balance: "This is the female century—over the last 40 years women have become the leading light in modern economies. They are filling the world's universities, starting more businesses and increasingly taking up positions of power."

A Deloitte Australia report on the workplace in 2030 echoed similar conclusions: "In a nutshell, we think that in the future, power will shift from institutions to individuals, and so it will be all about 'me.' But me, or rather 'we,' will look different--more sophisticated, educated, empowered and globally networked. We think that ideas will move between people not institutions. And in a borderless knowledge economy, powered by big data and global networks, insight will be the new currency and the concept that 'time is money' will be left behind."

Summary of Key Points:

- Many respected experts have observed that the free market style of Western capitalism is failing to produce economic and social security and well-being
- As a result of tumultuous economic conditions and technology, jobs as we knew them are disappearing and not likely to return
- The current workplace is characterized by increasing stress, lack of engagement and well-being for large numbers of employees
- Generation Y or the Millennials, by virtue of their numbers in the workplace come to work with values that reflect work-life balance, personal development and social conscience
- The well-being of employees, a new social contract and organizations that are equally committed to social and environmental good will need to become more widespread.

To get more resources regarding the future of work, Gen Y and the impact of technology, go to my website at: htt://raywilliams.ca

4 THE MIRACLE OF MINDFULNESS

I first stumbled into an awareness and practice of mindfulness out of necessity more than 20 years ago. By then I had been an executive and CEO already for more than two decades. But I was burnt out. My working life was characterized by long hours of work at least six days a week. My life was packed with meetings, interviews, discussions, telephone calls and conferences plugged into a calendar with no white space. And it was taking a toll on my personal life. I was spending less and less time and energy on my wife and children, and I had no time for myself.

And then I hit the wall. I got ill, and my employer became less enamored with me, so we parted company. I was physically and mentally exhausted and I had lost my passion for work, and most other things. Rather than immediately starting to look for a new job, I decided (and my doctors helped me make that decision) to take some substantial time off.

During the months that followed, I reflected on what had got me into that state of burn out, and I took the opportunity to not only be introspective, but also read about spirituality, emotional regulation and connecting with my inner self. It was the right decision. During this time, I became aware of the practices of meditation, became a practitioner, and have been ever since. As well, I read, and discussed with others the extended mindfulness practices focused on living a mindful life. I was hooked.

While it may sound a bit clichéd, mindfulness was a major factor in reclaiming my life and living a more meaningful life. As a result, the nature of the work I did, how I did it, and my relationships with others changed—for the better.

So those executives and professionals with whom I work will hear my personal passion when I encourage them to take up the mindful life.

What Is Mindfulness and Where Did It Come From?

Mindfulness in the meditative form has long historical roots in Hindu, Buddhist and Taoist religions and traditions. In Western culture, mindfulness grew out of many Jewish, Christian, Muslim and North American spiritual practices. For more than two decades, researchers, neuroscientists and mental health professionals have rediscovered these mindfulness traditions, seeing them as having promise for physical, mental and emotional well-being. Mindfulness is now spreading on a global scale throughout many institutions such as schools, prisons and hospitals, as well as businesses.

A Definition of Mindfulness

Most of the literature written about mindfulness refers to mindfulness meditation. In this book, I refer to informal mindfulness practices as well, that are not formal meditation. For the purposes of this book, references to mindfulness mean the formal meditative kind, unless I specifically refer to informal practices.

Jon Kabat-Zinn, founder of the Mindfulness-Based Stress Reduction Clinic at the University of Massachusetts Medical School, describes mindfulness as "paying attention in a particular way, on purpose, in the present moment and nonjudgmentally." Other definitions are: *"bringing one's complete attention to the present experience on a moment-to-moment basis,"* and *"it includes a quality of compassion, acceptance and loving-kindness."*

As we engage in mindful awareness practices, we have the potential to develop long-term personality traits from intentionally created mindful states. Research has suggested that these mindfulness traits include the capacity to suspend judgments; to act in awareness of our moment-to-moment experience; and to achieve emotional equilibrium or equanimity.

Mindfulness meditation comes in two distinct forms: formal meditation: when you intentionally take time out of your day to embark on a meditative practice; and informal meditation: when you go into a focused and "attentional" state of mind as you go about your daily activities.

Scientific Research on Mindfulness

More than 300 scientific studies have been completed on mindfulness, indicating its effectiveness and benefits. Here's a sample of some of the most significant studies:

- **Lasting emotional control.** Mindfulness meditation may make us feel calmer while we're doing it, but do these benefits spill over into everyday life? Gaelle Desbordes and colleagues published a study in the *Frontiers in Human Neuroscience*, in which they scanned the brains of people taking part in an 8-week meditation program, before and after the course. They found that meditation can help provide lasting emotional control, even when you are not meditating
- **Cultivating compassion.** In one study by Paul Condon and his colleagues, and published in *Psychological Science*, participants who had been meditating were given an undercover test of their compassion. They sat in a staged waiting area with two actors when another actor entered on crutches, pretending to be in great pain. The two actors sat next to the participants both ignored the person who was in pain, sending the unconscious signal not to intervene. Those who had been meditating, though, were 50% more likely to help the person in pain
- **Changes in brain structures.** Mindfulness meditation is such a powerful technique that, after only 8 weeks, the brain's structure changes. Research findings published in *Psychiatry Research*. Compared with a control group, grey-matter density in the hippocampus – an area associated with learning and memory–was increased. The study's lead author, Britta Hölzel, said: "It is fascinating to see the brain's plasticity and that, by practicing meditation, we can play an active role in changing the brain and can increase our well-being and quality of life"
- **Enhance cognitive functioning.** How would you like your brain to work faster? Fadel Zeidan and colleagues found significant benefits for novice meditators from only 80 minutes of meditation over four days. Their study was published in *Consciousness and Cognition*. The authors concluded "that four days of meditation training can enhance the ability to sustain attention; benefits that have previously been reported with long-term meditators." Improvements seen on the measures ranged from 15% to more than 50%
- **Sharpen concentration.** At its heart, meditation is all about learning to concentrate, to have greater control over the spotlight of attention. An increasing body of studies now underlines the benefits of meditation for attention. For example, researchers Amishi Jha and colleagues conducted a study, published in *Cognitive, Affective and Behavioral Sciences*, in which they sent 17 people who had not practiced meditation before they went on an 8-week training course in mindfulness-based stress reduction, a type of meditation.

These 17 participants were then compared with a further 17 from a control group on a series of attentional measures. The results showed that those who had received training were better at focusing their attention than the control group.

Other relevant research:

- Through the work of neuroscientist Richard Davidson and others, we've learned that people who practice mindful meditation regularly have higher levels of activity in the left prefrontal cortex of the brain, an area which is associated with personal growth and meaning. Davidson has shown that mindfulness meditation changes the brain including the development of greater cognitive flexibility and creativity, well-being, emotional regulation and empathy
- Researchers at the University of Massachusetts General Hospital, Harvard Medical School and MIT reported from their studies of that mindfulness practitioners were far more able to "turn down the volume" on distracting information and focus their attention better than non-mindfulness practitioners
- A study by Kirk Brown and Richard Ryan at the University of Rochester and published in the *Journal of Personality and Social Psychology*, found that people high on a mindfulness scale were more aware of their unconscious processes and had more cognitive control and greater ability to shape what they do and what they say, than people lower on the mindfulness scale. They also reported a mindfulness experience was positively associated with clarity of emotional states and mood, as well as higher levels of psychological well-being

What Are The Elements of Mindfulness?
Mindfulness, both in its formal meditative form and its informal activity based form comprise a number of elements which interact together to produce powerful brain, heart and behavioral changes. Here's a description of these elements:

1. **Being Present.** This means focusing your attention on whatever you are doing in the present moment. This implies you are not thinking about events or emotions from the past or in the future.
2. **Paying Attention.** Focusing 100% of your attention on whatever you are doing. The biggest single problem that contributes to mindlessness and prevents mindfulness is being on autopilot, which entails both not being present, and not noticing what you are

actually engaged in.

3. **Openness.** This involves both being open-minded in thought processes and openhearted in emotional activity. Practicing curiosity, "beginner's mind," and non-judgment are central to this element.

4. **Non-reactivity.** Our brains are built to have you react automatically, without thinking. Mindfulness encourages you to respond to your experience rather than react to your thoughts and emotions. Mindfulness is a deliberate and intentional choice.

5. **Acceptance.** This involves more than accepting other people the way they are, or accepting an event that has already happened. Its focus is on accepting and not practicing judgment or self-criticism about the thoughts, feelings, sensations, and beliefs that you have, and understanding that they are simply those things only.

6. **Compassion.** This element involves practicing compassion, empathy and kindness towards others and particularly toward yourself

7. **Non-attachment.** This element emphasizes avoidance of attaching meaning to thoughts and feelings, or connecting a given thought to a feeling. Instead, let a thought or feeling come in and pass without connecting it to anything, observing it exactly as they it is.

Are You Mindful? Take A Brief Self-Assessment
How many of the following things do you do?

Scoring: 5= I do this a lot; 4=I do this once and a while; 3=neutral; 2=I hardly ever do this; 1=I never do this.

1. ____ You run on automatic without much awareness of what you are doing.
2. ____ You rush through things without being attentive to them.
3. ____ You listen to someone with one ear, doing something else at the same time.
4. ____ You become preoccupied with the future or the past.
5. ____ You snack without being aware that you are eating.
6. ____ You get lost in your thoughts and feelings.
7. ____ Your mind wanders off and you are easily distracted.
8. ____ You drive on "automatic pilot" without paying attention to what you are doing.
9. ____ You daydream or think of other things when doing chore such as cleaning or handy work.
10. ____ You do several things at once rather than

focusing on one thing at a time.

11. ___ You criticize yourself when you fall behind in your tasks or goals.
12. ___ You are more interested in the finished product than the process of getting there.
13. ___ You don't forgive yourself or practice self compassion when you make a mistake.
14. ___ You believe you must do everything at 100%.
15. ___ You get impatient with other people or projects when they move "too slowly."
16. ___ You are reactive to other's criticism.
17. ___ You always physically move quickly or rush between appointments and meetings.
18. ___ You break or spill things.

Score: 60-90=You are not very mindful; 40-59=You are occasionally mindful; 18-39=You are mindful most of the time.

Myths About Mindfulness Meditation

Myth 1: Meditation is difficult. This myth is rooted in the image of meditation as an esoteric practice reserved for religious or spiritual people. When you receive instruction from an experienced, knowledgeable teacher, meditation is easy and fun to learn. The techniques can be as simple as focusing on the breath or silently repeating a mantra or phrase such as counting from one to ten. One reason why meditation may seem difficult is that you try too hard to concentrate, or you're overly attached to results, or you're not sure you are doing it right.

Myth 2: You have to quiet your mind in order to have a successful meditation practice. This may be the number one myth about meditation and is the cause of many people giving up in frustration. Meditation isn't about stopping your thoughts or trying to empty your mind – both of these approaches only create stress and more noisy internal chatter. You can't stop or control our thoughts, but you can decide how much attention to give them. Although you can't impose quiet on your mind, through meditation you can find the quiet that already exists in the space between your thoughts. This is sometimes referred to as "the gap," or the space. When you meditate, you use an object of attention, such as your breath, an image, or a mantra, which allows your mind to relax into this silent stream of awareness. When thoughts arise, as they inevitably will, you don't need to judge them or try to push them away. Instead, you can gently return your focus to your object of attention.

Be assured that even if it feels like you have been thinking throughout your entire meditation, you are still receiving the benefits of your practice. You haven't failed or wasted your time. Simply noticing that you are having thoughts is a breakthrough because it begins to shift your internal reference point from ego-mind to witnessing awareness. As you become less identified with your thoughts and stories, you experience greater peace and are open to new possibilities.

Myth 3: It takes years of dedicated practice to receive any benefits from meditation. The benefits of meditation are both immediate and long-term. You can begin to experience benefits the first time you sit down to meditate and in the first few days of daily practice. Many scientific studies provide evidence that meditation has profound effects on the mind-body physiology within just weeks of practice.

Myth 4: Meditation is escapism. The real purpose of meditation isn't to tune out and get away from it all but to tune in and get in touch with your true self – that eternal aspect of yourself that goes beyond all the ever-changing, external circumstances of your life. In meditation you dive below the mind's churning surface, which tends to be filled with repetitive thoughts about the past and worries about the future, into the still point of pure consciousness. In this state of awareness, you let go of all the stories you've been telling yourself about who you are, what is limiting you, and where you fall short.

As you practice on a regular basis, you cleanse the windows of perception and your clarity expands. While some people do try to use meditation as a form of escape – as a way to bypass unresolved emotional issues – this approach runs counter to all of the wisdom and scientific teachings about meditation and mindfulness.

Myth 5: You don't have enough time to meditate. There are busy, productive executives who have not missed a meditation in 25 years. If you make meditation a priority, you will do it. If you feel like your schedule is too full, remember that even just a few minutes of meditation is better than none. In life's paradoxical way, when you spend time meditating on a regular basis, you actually have more time. Your breathing and heart rate slow down, your blood pressure lowers, and your body decreases the production of stress hormones and other chemicals that speed up the aging process and give you the subjective feeling that we are "running out of time."

In meditation, you are in a state of restful alertness that is extremely refreshing for the body and mind. As people stick with their meditation ritual, they notice that they are able to accomplish more while doing less. Instead of struggling so hard to achieve goals, they spend more and more time "in the flow."

Myth 6: Meditation requires spiritual or religious beliefs. Meditation is a practice that takes us beyond the noisy chatter of the mind into stillness and silence. It doesn't require a specific spiritual belief, and many people of many different religions practice meditation without any conflict with their current religious beliefs. Some meditators have no particular religious beliefs or are atheist or agnostic. They meditate in order to experience inner quiet and the numerous physical and mental health benefits of the practice – including lowered blood pressure, stress reduction, and restful sleep.

What Do You Do In Meditation?
What is it that we do during meditation? Simply put, we're doing a few basic things:

- **We're bringing our attention to the present moment**. By doing this, we start to lose our tendency to lose focus on what's going on around us and spend time in a past we can't change, or a future that we can't reliably depend on
- **We observe what's happening in that moment**. This starts to weaken our habit of mistakenly identifying ourselves as our body, feelings, thoughts, or that which is going on around us
- **We set aside judgment about what we observe**. This helps us disengage from the narratives which often guide our actions, instead of us guiding our actions
- **We can then narrow the focus of our attention to a single object, or widen it to encompass a variety of phenomenon, all still in the present moment.** Whatever particular technique we use, we're developing skills that help us *respond* better during the challenges of daily living, rather than *reacting* out of the usual habit patterns, likes, aversions, emotions, or train of thoughts.

Where and When
Set aside a location and time, perhaps somewhere quiet in your home, where you won't be disturbed while you're meditating. If you can find a spot that's going to allow you to be physically comfortable, calm, where you can set aside the stresses of the day, that might be a good place to consider. Turn off your cell phone, and try to arrange with others in the house to let you have a little uninterrupted time to yourself. If others can be quiet, too,

it can help to have as few distractions as possible. You may want to have a timer, so something else can keep track of how long you meditate and you can focus on present moment awareness. Pick one that has a gentle, rather than jarring tone when the set time is up, to let you know this session's set time is complete without startling you, and one that doesn't tick or make any noise while you're practicing.

Step-By-Step Meditation Instructions
Once you've got an understanding of the ideas of what you're doing in meditation, your location is picked out, and you have a time when you can meditate undisturbed, the next step is to give it a try.

You don't have to sit on a cushion, you can sit in a chair. If you do, it can help you remain alert by sitting forward, not leaning on the back rest, but fully alert, attentive, maintaining an upright posture. You can rest your hands in your lap, in a position that won't cause tension in your shoulders or neck. Be sure to set your timer for whatever is a manageable, but set a goal, and start it. If it's your first time, ten minutes is a reasonable starting point. It may be helpful for you to start with two things. First, *set an intention* for this session. That intention may be to put aside your stresses from the day, it may be to keep your attention on the object of your meditation, or to move your awareness through various places on your body. Second, *relax and attend* to the present moment, perhaps by taking three very slow, deep breaths, inviting your awareness to the sensation of the breath.

The breath is what you can start with. It is always there for you, even when you're not meditating, and is a very useful way to develop attention in this simple activity in the present moment. You can direct your awareness to the sensation of air passing at the tip of your nose, or the expansion of your belly, whichever is easiest for you to notice and follow. Have an open and relaxed, inquisitive attitude about this simple physical process; be aware of the starting of the in-breath, through the entire duration of the inhale, up to the end; then switching to the out-breath, its arising, its duration; and then completion. Invite the attention afresh with the next breath, and the one after that, just observing the sensation.

Feel the sensation of your breath as it flows in and out of your nostrils at the tip of your nose. Some people feel the sensation more strongly within the nostrils, while others feel it more on the upper lip. To help you locate where you feel the touch sensation of the breath most distinctly, inhale deeply and force the air out through your nostrils. Wherever you feel the sensation most clearly and precisely is the place to focus your attention for the balance of the meditation period. If you can't stay with this small target, shift to feeling the rise and fall of your abdomen or chest.

Feel the beginning, the middle, and the end of every in-breath, and the beginning, the middle, and the end of every out-breath and be present with the pauses in between. Sometimes the breath will be short—there is no need to make it longer. Sometimes the breath will be long—there is no need to make it shorter. Sometimes the breath will be erratic—there is no need to make it even or smooth. Just become aware of the breath as it goes in and out of the nostrils at the tip of the nose. Let the breath breathe itself. Every time your attention moves away from the breath and shifts to another physical sensation, sound, smell or thought, gently but firmly bring your attention back to the touch sensation of your breath.

At first what seems like a new and increased number of thoughts can easily distract us, but they're not new, we're simply stepping back and noticing them perhaps for the first time in our lives. It's not a problem, they've always been there, and they not only lack substance, but each one arises and falls, just like the breath. They're impermanent, coming and going, and you can start to build a skill in your meditation of just letting them be thoughts instead of powerful ideas upon which you have to act. Every moment, you have a choice, and meditation helps you begin to notice that and make the best choice you can.

If you lose track of the breath, that's okay, and is in fact very normal and expected. Don't beat yourself up about it, just kindly and gently return your attention to the breath. You'll do this again and again, throughout the entire meditation session. This is what we mean by the practice.

There are many ways to help you apply your attention and sustain it. One way to do this is to count with each exhale, starting with one, put your full attention on the inhale, then count silently two to yourself on the next exhale, put your full attention on the next inhale… all the way to ten. After reaching ten, start again at one. Again, it's perfectly normal and expected to lose count! Just kindly and gently return your attention to the breath, and start again at one.

As you continue with a regular meditation practice, over time you may be able to maintain an unbroken count to ten for the entire meditation session of ten minutes. If you can do that consistently, consider increasing the amount of time you meditate to fifteen, twenty, or thirty minutes. Even if you can't maintain the count to ten, if you can meditate for longer than ten minutes, try increasing the amount of time.

You can then consider challenging your attention by just counting to one. That may sound easy, but can be even harder than counting to ten! And eventually, drop the counting entirely from your meditation — it's not about the count, it's about developing your ability to apply and maintain your attention. Eventually your awareness of the breath can come more easily, and instead of having to continually bring it back, the thoughts can settle more quickly and consistently, so your attention is maintained without putting forth as much effort.

Meditation isn't about the meditation itself, it's about building a skill that we can take out into the world. We develop both concentration and awareness so we're able to more frequently recognize what's happening right *now*, make more intentional decisions about where our attention should be, and respond to daily situations in a more skillful way.

Informal Ways of Being Mindful
Informal ways of being mindful can strengthen and augment formal meditation and reinforce the elements of mindfulness described before in the book. Informal mindfulness involves focusing your attention in the present moment in a curious, open-minded, non-judgmental way as you go about your daily activities, no matter how mundane and ordinary they may be. The following are some examples.

Mindful Walking. Typically, when we walk somewhere the focus is on the destination. We see walking as the means to getting somewhere and achieving an end or goal, such as getting to a meeting, going shopping, or even walking in the park to arrive at a particular place. Mindful walking is different. The focus is on the journey with no destination in mind. And in the process, our minds focus on the physical sensations of walking—how it feels in different parts of our body, and what feelings that generates in us. The following is a description of the process and what to expect:

- Stand on the spot, being aware of your weight being transferred through the soles of your feet into the earth or the floor. Be aware of all of the subtle movements that go on in order to keep you balanced and upright
- Walk very slowly so you feel the roll of your feet. Keep your attention on the soles of your feet; be aware of the alternating patterns of contact and release; be aware of your foot as the heel first makes contact, as your foot rolls forward onto the ball, and then lifts and travels through the air
- Be aware of all the different sensations in your feet, not just a contact in the soles of your feet but the contact between the toes,

the feeling of the inside of your shoes, the fabric of your socks, and let your feet be as relaxed as you can. Be aware of your ankles. Notice the qualities of the sensations in those joints – as your foot is on the ground, as your foot travels through the air

- Let your ankle joints be relaxed. Be aware of your lower legs – your shins, your calves. Be aware of the contact with your clothing. Be aware of the temperature on your skin
- Notice what the calf muscles are doing as you're walking. You might even want to exaggerate for a few steps what the calf muscles are doing, and then let your walking go back to a normal relaxed rhythm. Encourage your calf muscles to be relaxed
- Be aware of your knees--notice the qualities of the sensations in your knee joints. Then expand your awareness into your thighs. Be aware of the skin, again the contact with your clothing, the temperature. Be aware of the muscles, and notice what the muscles on the fronts of the thighs, and the muscles on the backs of the thighs are doing
- Exaggerate what those muscles are doing – exaggerate the action of those muscles. Be aware of your hips – the muscles around your hip joints — and relaxing those muscles. Really relax. Even when you think you've relaxed – relax them some more
- Notice how that changes your walk. Notice how the rhythm and the gait of your walk change as your hips relax. Be aware of the whole of your pelvis – and notice all of the movements that are going on your pelvis. One hip moves forward and then the other; one hip lifting, the other sinking
- Be aware of the complex three-dimensional shape that your pelvis is carving out through space as you walk forwards. The lowest part of your spine – your sacrum – is embedded in the pelvis. So as you feel your spine extending upwards – the lumbar spine, the thoracic spine – you can notice how it moves along with the pelvis. Your spine is in constant motion. It's swaying from side to side. There is a twisting motion around the central axis. Your spine is in constant, sinuous, sensuous motion
- Notice your belly – you might feel your clothing in contact with your belly – and notice how your belly is the center of your body. Very often it feels like it's "down there" because we are so much in our heads. So seek to what extent you can feel your belly is the center of your body, as the center of your being. Notice your chest, and just let your breathing happen. Notice the contact that your chest makes with your clothing
- Notice your shoulders. Let your shoulders be relaxed, and let your shoulders passively transmit the rhythm of your walk down into

your arms. Let your arms simply hanging by your sides and swinging naturally. Notice all the motions in your arms – your upper arms, your elbows, your forearms, your wrists, your hands. And feel the air coursing over the skin on your hands and fingers as your arms swing through the air

- Be aware of your neck – and the muscles supporting your skull. Notice the angle of your head. And notice that as you relax the muscles on the back of your neck, your chin slightly tucks in and your skull comes to a point of balance. And you might want to play around with the angle of your head and see how it changes your experience. You might notice that when you tuck your chin close into your chest, your experience becomes darker and more emotional – that you're more inward turned, somber. And if you lift your chin and hold it in the air you might notice that your experience becomes much lighter – that you become much more aware of the outside world and perhaps caught up in the outside world, or much more aware of your thoughts and caught up in your thoughts. And then, bringing your head back to a point of balance, your chin slightly tucked in

- Relax your jaw. Relax your eyes — and just let your eyes be softly focused, gently looking ahead – not staring at anything, not allowing yourself to be caught up in anything that's going past you

- Be aware of the feelings that you're having; not in terms of emotions here, but just the feeling tone. Are there things that feel pleasant; are there things that feel unpleasant – in your body, or outside of you? So if you notice things in your body that are pleasant or unpleasant, just notice them. Don't cling onto them, or push them away, but just notice them. If you notice things in the outside world that are either pleasant or unpleasant, just allow them to drift by – just notice them to drift by without following them or averting your gaze from them

- Notice your emotional states. Are you bored? Are you content? Are you irritated? Are you feeling very happy to be doing what you're doing? Again just noticing whatever emotions happen to be present. And notice your mind also. Is your mind clear, or dull? Is your mind busy, or is it calm? Are you thinking about things unconnected with this practice – or do whatever thoughts that you have center on what you're doing just now? Just notice these things with no particular judgment

- Notice the balance between your experience of the inner and the outer. Be aware of both the inner world and the outer world in equal balance, so your mind settles at a point of stillness, and calmness, and clarity. So see if you can find that point of balance, where you're equally aware of the inner and the outer, and your mind is calm, content, and quiet

- Come to a natural halt. You're not freezing on the spot; you're just allowing yourself to come to a stop. And just experience yourself standing. Just notice what it's like to no longer be in motion. Notice once more the complex balancing act that's going on to keep you upright. Feeling once again, the weight traveling down through the soles of your feet into the earth; simply standing, and experiencing yourself and, finally, bringing this meditation session to a close.

Mindful Daily Routines

Here's some other routines that present an opportunity for you to practice being mindful. Daily consistent practice will help you master mindfulness more quickly and help you move from being on autopilot to being more aware of your environment and your internal state.

1. **Mindful Eating**. Mindful eating involves paying full attention to the experience of eating and drinking, both inside and outside the body.
   - Pay attention to the colors, smells, textures, flavors, temperatures, and even the sounds (crunch!) of your food. Pay attention to the experience of the body. Where in the body do we feel hunger? Where do you feel satisfaction? What does half-full feel like, or three-quarters full?
   - Pay attention to the mind. While avoiding judgment or criticism, watch when the mind gets distracted, pulling away from full attention to what you are eating or drinking. Watch the impulses that arise after you've taken a few sips or bites: to grab a book, to turn on the TV, to call someone on our cell phone, or to do web search on some interesting subject
   - Notice the impulse and return to just eating. Notice how eating affects your mood and how your emotions like anxiety influence our eating. Gradually you regain the sense of ease and freedom with eating that you had in childhood. The old habits of eating and not paying attention are not easy to change. Don't try to make drastic changes. Lasting change takes time, and is built on many small changes. Start simply
   - Give yourself mindful eating homework. Try taking the first four sips of a cup of hot tea or coffee with full attention. If you are reading and eating, try alternating

these activities, not doing both at once. Read a page, then put the book down and eat a few bites, savoring the tastes, then read another page, and so on. At family meals, you might ask everyone to eat in silence for the first five minutes, thinking about the many people who brought the food to your plates. Try eating one meal a week mindfully, alone and in silence. Be creative. For example, could you eat lunch behind a closed office door, or even alone in your car?

2. **Mindful Driving.** Driving can be a very stressful activity, but it can also be a tremendous opportunity for developing mindfulness and it can even become a kind of meditation practice in its own right. Obviously, when you're driving it's not recommended that you close your eyes and focus on your breathing. So here are a few suggestions that you can use driving as a meditation:

- Switch off the radio and experience the silence. We often drive along while listening to the radio or to a CD. Just as an experiment, try seeing what it's like to have the sound turned off. It might seem at first as if something is missing, but you'll quickly learn that the silence gives you an opportunity to fill your awareness with other perceptions, some of which are more enriching. Stopping listening to advertisements, the news, music, and opinion can leave you quieter, calmer, more focused, and happier than you otherwise would be
- The extra attention that's freed up because you're no longer listening to the radio is now available to notice other things. You can notice any tensions in your body, such as a knot of tension in the belly, or your hands gripping the steering wheel, or a clenched jaw. Notice these experiences, and let your body relax more. Notice how your experience changes and becomes more enjoyable as your muscles let go
- Slow down. As an experiment, try driving at or just below the speed limit. Most of us tend to want to push the speed limit, driving just a little faster than allowed. Driving just a fraction under the speed limit can take away a lot of tension. Shift over into the slower lane if necessary
- Notice your attitudes. Often we become competitive while driving, and this leads to tension. Make a practice of noticing cars trying to enter the road, and adjust your

speed so that you can let them out if it's safe to do so. Notice if you're in a hurry. How does this make you feel? How does it feel if you let the pace slacken a little?

- Use every stoplight or any other necessary stop to practice a fuller mindfulness of your body. When you've stopped, it's safe to let your awareness more fully connect with your breathing. At those moments you can also notice what's around you — the sky and the trees, and other people
- As you get into your car, before you switch on the engine, and before you get out of the car, just sit for a moment and take three deep breaths, really letting go on the out breath
- When you get into the car, turn off your mobile phone, or at least silence it. Turn off the vibrate function as well

3. Some Other Informal Routines Providing An Opportunity For Mindfulness

There's no shortage of daily routine activities that can provide opportunities for mindfulness. The keys here, regardless of the activities, are to slow down, bring your full attention to what you are doing, use your senses to enjoy the experience and be present. This can be done while getting up in the morning, taking a shower, brushing your teeth, getting dressed, doing house chores or handyman projects, preparing meals, etc. Make sure you focus on the details of what you doing. Notice what are the colors, smells, feel, and other characteristics of your activities.

Who You Are And Who You Are Not

An essential component of mindfulness is making a separation between you and your thoughts and emotions, which are chemical-electrical activities going on in your brain. If "you" were indistinguishable from your body, thoughts or feelings, then you would never leave the state you are in. You would be perpetually in that state. Here are the things you are not:

- **You are not your body.** Your body is made up of hundreds of millions of cells that are dying and being replaced constantly. The atoms in the cells are exchanging with atoms in your environment all the time. You are neither conscious of all this activity nor in control of it
- **You are not your thoughts.** Thoughts keep coming, no matter how much you meditate. If you were your thoughts, it wouldn't be possible to observe them. And if your were your thoughts, you'd be able to predict what thought you are going to have next. The fact

56

that you can observe your thoughts means they're separate and a space lies between you and what you think. In mindfulness, you can step back from your thoughts from time to time, but you can't control your thoughts, you can only be aware of them. You can also choose what to focus your attention on, which in a sense determines the nature of what your thoughts are

- **You are not your emotions**. You can also observe your emotions. Emotions arise and can pass away. Again, if you were your emotions, you wouldn't be able to observe them.

So if you are not your body, and not your thoughts, and not your emotions, what's left?

You are the observer or the witness. And if you're that, you can't be the thing you are observing or witnessing. You are awareness, presence, being, consciousness. Thoughts, ideas, actions arise in you, and you're aware of all of them.

The Difference Between Doing and Being
The doing mode is highly developed in people, particularly Western culture. We think about how we want things to be and then take action steps to make it happen. Many of us are in a constant state of activity, trying to accomplish something, moving toward a destination, achieving a goal, being busy.

Mindfulness encourages a being mode of living, where there is nothing to accomplish, and yet you are fully aware of what is going on around you and in you. Every day in every thing you do, your mind switches between doing mode and being mode. Both are required for healthy living. Unfortunately, the doing mode dominates our lives. We are continually accomplishing goals, tasks, timelines, jobs with our focus on the future. Mindfulness presents the opportunity to strengthen the being mode, which is important for mental and emotional health.

Here's the difference between the two modes of mind:

Doing	Being
• You are aware of how things are and how they should be; • You set a goal to fix the things that are missing or "wrong"; • You try harder and harder to	• You connect with the present moment every day; • You acknowledge and allow things to be as they are, rather than trying to change the past;

achieve the goal; • Most of your actions happened automatically, without conscious awareness; • You are not connected to the present moment, and are more likely focused on the past or future; • You increasingly speed up your activity; • You try to accomplish too many things at once; • You become disconnected from your body; • You are not aware of your emotions, and focus mostly on your thinking.	• You're open to pleasant, unpleasant and neutral emotions without judgment; • You have an inner sense of awareness, peace, stillness and silence; • You are very focused and attentive to whatever you are doing, no matter how trivial; • You avoid multi-tasking; • You intentionally choose how to act, speak, think and feel; • You are conscious of your physical state at all times; • You bring an element of compassion including self-compassion into your life.

Dealing With Your Emotions in the Being Mode

If you're in a doing mode, and you experience an emotion such as anger or sadness, you might be prompted to solve it, get out of it. Doing mode can send your mind into a spin, causing many negative thoughts. The next time you feel an uncomfortable feeling like sadness, anger, frustration or jealous, try this exercise to get into a being mode:

- Set your intention. Let your intention be to feel the emotion and its effects as best you can with curiosity. You're just creating a space for it without needing to run away or make it go away
- Feel the emotion. Feel it with care, kindness and acceptance. Open up to it. Notice where the emotion manifests itself in your body
- Breathe into that part of your body and stay with it
- Allow the emotion to be as it is. You don't need to fight or run away
- De-center from the emotion. Notice you can be aware of the emotion without being the emotion itself. Create a space between you and the feeling. Observe it as though you are watching it from a distance
- Breathe. Simply feel your breath, and notice it in your body

Living The Mindful Life

Mindfulness is more than meditative practice, although that is the necessary cornerstone. It's also about a way of being and a way of living that can bring greater happiness, health and well-being. It's about daily practices that permeate your work and personal life. It's about building routines in your life that are as fundamental as brushing your teeth and breathing. Here's a comprehensive list to tell if you're becoming more mindful. Keep this list handy for regular reference and a progress check.

How To Tell if you're becoming more mindful:

1. You notice that you are becoming less judgmental of yourself and others.
2. You develop curiosity about things that you used to deny or judge as "wrong," "stupid," or "impossible."
3. You accept your partner, family members and friends just as they are and give up trying to change them, improve them or persuade them to your perspective.
4. You're willing to admit you may not be right, and honestly want to hear others' perspectives, rather than needing to prove they are "wrong".
5. Your "black and white" opinions about the world soften and you become allowing/tolerant of differing views, cultures and societies.
6. You don't spend most of your time thinking about the past or the future, but rather focus on the present.
7. You let go of the need for perfection and accept yourself as you are, including your imperfections.
8. You feel compassion for every living thing, even those who you don't naturally "like".
9. You are not reactive to others' actions; they can't push triggers or buttons in you that result in a lack of control over your emotions.
10. When you need to respond to others' actions or words, you do so intentionally, thoughtfully and in control of your emotions.
11. You accept your emotions--including your negative emotions--and the "shadow" in yourself as being part of you, and don't let that part rule you.
12. You are patient. You understand that all things must develop in their own time, and that you can't "force" things to happen.
13. You have trust in yourself. You trust yourself, your intuition and your abilities, including your ability to get through everything.
14. You commit yourself to non-striving. You accept things that are happening in the moment just as they are supposed to be. You don't spend time wishing things were different or trying to relive the past differently.

15. You don't try to run away from pain, but rather embrace it as part of life, which will lessen its negative effect. You understand that suffering arises from your resistance to pain. You understand that whatever you resist persists.
16. You understand that consciously setting your intentions for your life, your thinking, and your behavior without being attached to outcomes is necessary to being mindful.
17. You are aware that body and mind are one, and that you are aware of your internal physical state at all times, but particularly during stressful times.
18. You focus on the things that you have with gratitude rather than focusing on the things you don't have.
19. You accept the universe and that everything in it is constantly changing. Nothing lasts forever, and nothing stays the same.
20. You spend some private quiet time every day.
21. You practice self-compassion consistent with the compassion you show others.

Summary of Key Points:

- Mindfulness provides people with the opportunity to be more present, focused and healthy
- Mindfulness comprises both formal meditation practice and informal daily routine practices
- Scientific studies demonstrate the health, emotional and behavioral benefits of mindfulness mediation
- Mindfulness meditation can be an effective way of dealing with the stresses of life and work
- Mindfulness is a way of life, not just a particular technique or skill.

To get more resources of the nature of mindfulness including meditative and informal practices, go to my website: http://raywilliams.ca

5 WHAT DO WE KNOW ABOUT LEADERSHIP TODAY?

Early in my career, the conventional wisdom and theories of leadership that I was exposed to and believed in had been around a long time. The leaders I met and was given as a model to emulate was a typical stereotype, and to a large extent, still exists. That stereotype was as follows:

- A white, middle-aged male who was tall and masculine looking
- A personality that came across as confident, often aggressive, and condescending to females
- Someone who was decisive, and predominantly action-oriented
- A leadership style that was clearly command-and-control often with overtones of the military or professional sports
- Someone who was somewhat aloof or distant from followers or employees

In my naiveté as a young leader, I believed I needed to exhibit those characteristics (except being tall and middle aged) and I did my best to look like the stereotype. And I achieved success if success can be measured by getting promotions. Yet there was something missing in the stereotype, something that in the ensuing years I sought to find. I became a student of studying leadership in biographies, descriptions and theories by management experts, to find what was missing. The answers eventually came to me as two things—self-mastery, and leading from the heart.

Following is a brief summary of the various theories of leadership that will help focus on how mindful leadership is different.

Theories of Leadership
Plato once said that the human race would have no rest from its evils until philosophers became kings or kings became philosophers. Perhaps there is

another option, as increasing numbers of people are assuming leadership of their own lives. They become their own central power. As the Scandinavian proverb says, "In each of us there is a king. Speak to him and he will come forth."

Few subjects have been researched and written about more than leadership. A recent Google search on the word leadership turns up over 500,000,000 entries. A search on Amazon yields more than 80,000 books on the topic and there have been millions of articles published on the subject.

The dictionary defines leadership as "the position or function of a leader, a person who guides or directs a group", a definition that is exceedingly vague and general. Leadership has been described by Martin Chemers in his book, *An Integrative Theory of Leadership* as "a process of social influence in which one person can enlist the aid and support of others in the accomplishment of a common task". For example, some people understand a leader simply as somebody whom people follow, or as somebody who guides or directs others, while others define leadership as "organizing a group of people to achieve a common goal".

The search for the characteristics or traits of leaders has been ongoing for centuries. Philosophical writings from Plato's *Republic* to Plutarch's *Lives* have explored the question "What qualities distinguish an individual as a leader?" Underlying this search was the early recognition of the importance of leadership and the assumption that leadership is rooted in the characteristics that certain individuals possess.

As early as 500 years Before Christ the concept of leadership was debated. At that time, the Chinese philosopher Confucius recognized some virtues of effective leaders. There were four cornerstones to his belief namely: *Jen*= love; *Li* = proper conduct; *Xiao* = piety; *Zhang rong* = moderation.

It is striking that three of the four virtues are emotional and just one is managerial. Aristotle's view of pathos, ethos, and logos is similar to Confucius in the sense that he also identifies both emotional and managerial values. According to Aristotle a leader must build relationships with those who are led.

While history is filled with references to great leaders such as Alexander the Great or Abraham Lincoln, more formal leadership theories emerged in the 20th century. These theories can be summarized as follows.

"Great Men" or "Heroic" Theory

Do you believe that some people are just born to lead? That's the basis behind this early 20th century theory proposed by Thomas Carlyle. Carlyle believed that history could largely be explained through the actions of "great men", individuals who he believed exerted high levels of influence over others through their inborn charisma, intelligence, wisdom, or drive for power. According to this theory, genetics were accountable for leaders. The individual was "born to lead". Leaders were often portrayed as heroic and even mythical. This theory assumed great leaders, Joan of Arc not withstanding, were male, and usually exhibited military accomplishments.

Trait Theory

Do you believe that all great leaders share the same traits? Similar to the Great Men Theory, trait theories assume that people have certain qualities that make them better suited to leadership, even if they are not inherited. Particular personality characteristics such as extraversion, self-confidence and courage are illustrative. The argument for this theory is correlational— i.e., examples of great leaders who exhibit these qualities are often profiled.

The difficulty with the argument is that many people who may exhibit these traits have not become leaders. And many people who don't exhibit these characteristics have become leaders. The biggest criticism of trait theory is that the traits are often poor predictors of behavior, and the theory does not allow for individual differences.

While researchers initially thought there was great promise in this theory, studies would go on to show that there were no universal traits that consistently separated effective leaders from other individuals, though this may have been in part to blame on poor methodology on the part of the researchers. Yet these findings do bring up some interesting points and also showcase just how hard it is to pin down what separates good leaders from bad ones.

Situational Theories

Does great leadership depend on the situation? Situational theories of leadership focus on variables in the environment that might determine which particular style of leadership is best suited to the situation. According to this theory, no one leadership style is best in all situations. Situational theories propose that leaders choose the best course of action based upon situational variables.

Different styles of leadership and decision-making may be determined by the situation or event. A way of looking at this would be to consider the ship is sinking. An authoritarian style of leadership may be better in a crisis situation whereas a more democratic one may be more effective in working with highly skilled teams not in a crisis. Situational theories of leadership generally propose that leaders choose the best course of action based on variables that change from situation to situation.

This theory was first proposed by Dr. Paul Hersey and Dr. Ken Blanchard, who believed that leaders chose their leadership style based on the maturity or level of the follower, dividing up the necessary leadership behaviors into four different quadrants. These included directing, coaching, supporting, and delegating, in order of those that provide the most supervision and direction to those that require the least. The fundamental lesson of this theory is that there is no one "best" style of leadership, and to truly be effective, leaders has to change and adapt their methods depending on the situation and the person or group they're working with.

Contingency Theory
Are there multiple factors that account for great leaders? Proposed by Dr. Fred Fiedler, this theory states that the best leadership style isn't set in stone but varies depending on a given situation, meaning that some leaders simply may not be a good fit for certain environments. Fiedler developed the Least Preferred Coworker Scale as a way to determine which managers would be the best fit for a leadership assignment. In order to determine whether a leader is favorable for a given task, Fiedler examined three factors: the leader-member relationship, the degree of task structure, and the leader's position power. If all three of these dimensions are high, the leader, and his or her leadership style, is considered a favorable match. For example, a leader with a drill sergeant-like attitude probably isn't the best choice for an office that requires creative thinking and collaboration.

Behavioral Theory
Can we judge great leaders based on their behavior only? The Behavioral Theory of leadership is based upon the belief that great leaders are made, not born. Rooted in behavioral psychology, the theory focuses on the actions of the leader, not their mental qualities or internal states.
In response to the early criticisms of the trait approach, theorists began to research leadership as a set of behaviors, evaluating the behavior of successful leaders, determining behavior taxonomy, and identifying broad leadership styles. David McClelland, for example, posited that leadership takes a strong personality with a well-developed positive ego. To lead, self-confidence and high self-esteem are useful, perhaps even essential. Kurt Lewin, Ronald Lipitt, and Ralph White developed in 1939 the seminal work

on the influence of leadership styles and performance.

The managerial grid model is also based on a behavioral theory. The model was developed by Robert Blake and Jane Mouton in 1964 and suggests five different leadership styles, based on the leaders' concern for people and their concern for goal achievement.

Charismatic Theory

Are all great leaders charismatic and extraverted? In Greek "charisma" means "divinely inspired gift". Max Weber was the first to describe charismatic leadership. He described characteristics such as mystical, narcissistic, and a personal magnetic savior who would arise to lead people through crises. House developed a theory of charismatic leadership that defines charisma in terms of its effects.

Participative Theory

Do great leaders encourage the participation of their followers? Participative Leadership Theory arises from the work of Dr. Rensis Likert in 1967. Likert proposed several types of leadership styles including exploitative authoritative, benevolent authoritative, consultative, and participative. Participative leaders were those who show great concern for employees and use input and advice from these individuals when making decisions.

A similar theory was proposed by Dr. Gary Yukl in 1971, with the leadership style being called delegative rather than participative. Today, the ability to be seen as a participative leader can still be important and those in leadership positions who don't take the thoughts and feelings of their subordinates into account are rarely regarded as truly great leaders. Participative Theories suggest that the ideal leadership style requires the input from others. The leader's job is to encourage participation in the decision-making process.

Authentic Theory

Are great leaders just "being themselves"? Authentic Leadership Theory is relatively new, coming onto the scene in 2008 when it was coined by researchers Bruce Avolio and Fred Luthans, and it's undoubtedly a term you've heard in business or leadership literature before. At the heart of the Authentic Leadership Theory is the idea that leaders should demonstrate a pattern of behavior that promotes a healthy work environment, both mentally and physically; creates an ethical climate; fosters self-awareness; is transparent; and offers an internal moral perspective. That's a tall order, but one that many businesses, some hopelessly focused on profit over personnel, may need to find in management to help retain and motivate employees.

Emotional Intelligence Theory

Do great leaders have higher levels of emotional intelligence? Emotional Intelligence Theory is linked to job performance and leader effectiveness. Daniel Goleman, author of *Emotional Intelligence*, argues that leaders are alike in one crucial way, in that they all have a high degree of emotional intelligence (EQ). In Goleman's opinion leaders obviously need a high intelligence level (IQ) and sufficient technical kills and knowledge.

However, these are the minimal requirements for being a leader. Emotional intelligence is what makes the difference between a leader and an effective leader according to this school of thought. There are three groups of capabilities; technical, cognitive, and emotional intelligence capabilities. Goleman identified five personal capabilities that emotionally intelligent people posses: self-awareness; self-regulation; motivation; empathy; and social skill.

Transformational or Relational Theories

Can we judge great leadership by the results of their work on their organizations? These theories focus on the connection between leaders and followers. Transformational leaders motivate and inspire people by supporting them to a higher good or common goal. These leaders also want each person to fulfill their potential and these leaders have high ethical and moral standards. Transformational leadership is about managing energy, first in yourself and then in those around you. Transformational leaders represent the high moral road of leadership involving unique bonds among leaders and followers. Transformational leaders are very much like coaches and mentors.

It has been the subject of countless books, articles, and academic investigations from the 1980s up to the present day, including a seminal work on the theory by James McGregor Burns in 1978. According to Burns, transformational leadership exists in opposition to transactional leadership. Where transactional leadership is superficial, transformational leadership is a process by which real, lasting changes are made in both followers and raise one another to higher levels of morality and motivation.

Servant Theory

Do great leaders act as servants to their followers? In 1977, Robert Greenleaf published a series of essays on a new type of leadership that he coined "servant leadership." Servant leadership is focused on the follower, not the leader, and encourages those in leadership positions to pay close attention to the needs, desires, and motivations of subordinates. His work would be the inspiration for Larry Spears, who broke Greenleaf's leadership model down into ten characteristics every servant leader must have. These include: listening, empathy, healing, awareness, persuasion, conceptualization, foresight, stewardship, commitment to growth, and commitment to building a community. With organizations across the nation trying to build more transparent and ethical leadership strategies in the wake of numerous scandals, this theory of leadership has received increased attention and should be something every well-rounded leader learns more about.

Values-based Theory
In simple terms, values-based leadership is leading by staying true to one's values. It means to lead others by remaining consistent with the leader's beliefs and never swaying from one's fundamental values. The leader may change his or her strategy, tactics, or approach given the situation, but the leader never changes his or her underlying values, beliefs, or principles. Values-based leadership is based on the notion that personal and organizational values are aligned.

A company's mission, vision, strategy, performance measures, incentive programs, procedures, and values are all a representation of the leader's ethics and values. This approach to leadership assumes that managers' and workers' core principles are the same; therefore, little time is spent on office conflict. This also means that employees and managers behave in a way that is conducive to the productivity, profitability, sustainability, and integrity of the business.

Spiritual Theory
Does a great leader need to be driven by deep spiritual beliefs? This theory comes from the view that organizations must care for the employee's physical, emotional, as well as spiritual well-being. Some companies are encouraging meaningful work by combining their profit motive with the values of social responsibility. Encouraging employees' spirit of accomplishment and motivation, by the idea that the company supplies a reasonable amount of money to charity. However, to encourage the spirituality in the workplace, leaders have to take on a different leadership style. Understanding workplace spirituality begins with acknowledging that people have both an inner and an outer life, and that nourishment of the inner life can lead to a more meaningful and productive outer life.

Is There Common Agreement Now Among Experts?

While there is not unanimous agreement among scholars and leadership experts, it would be fair to say that transformational, servant, emotional intelligence and values-based leadership have the strongest credibility at this point.

What's particularly interesting about these leadership theories is the gap between what researchers recognize as the elements of effective leadership and good leaders and what the general public perceives. There still is a predominant general view both inside and outside organizations that leadership traits and competencies best describe what good leaders do and a command-and-control style of leadership still is predominant.

The Current Crisis In Leadership

Leadership is in a storm, a storm that is gathering and threatens to contribute to the decay of our institutions and economic and social structures. As many observers have noted, we are in a crisis of leadership. Let's look first at this leadership storm and what leads one to conclude we're in a leadership crisis.

In the past two decades, 30% of Fortune 500 CEOs have lasted less than 3 years. Top executive failure rates are as high as 75% and rarely less than 30%. Chief executives now are lasting 7.6 years on a global average down from 9.5 years in 1995.

According to the *Harvard Business Review*, 2 out of 5 new CEOs fail in their first 18 months on the job. It appears that the major reason for the failure has nothing to do with competence, or knowledge, or experience, but rather with hubris and ego. According to the *National Leadership Index* report, 75% of organizations reported a deficit of leadership skills. Forty-two per cent of managers rate their own line-manager as ineffective; 70% of Americans still believe they have a crisis of leadership. What's more 70% agree that unless leadership improves, the U.S. will decline as a nation.

Research shows when someone assumes a new or different leadership role they have a 40% chance of demonstrating disappointing performance. Furthermore, 82% of newly appointed leaders derail because they fail to build partnerships with subordinates and peers. Public poll after public poll has shown that people have lost confidence in our political and business leaders. Why? Let's look at some research that may provide some answers.

Ego, Hubris And Loss Of Trust

Why do employees quit their jobs, and have problems with engagement? Leigh Branham, author of *7 Hidden Reasons Employees Leave*, analyzed over 20,000 anonymous surveys asking employees why they left their last job. Although most managers believe pay is the primary reason people quit, Branham discovered that the number one reason actually is "loss of trust and confidence in senior leaders." And that loss of trust is often correlated to abusive bosses.

Harvard Business School Professor Gautama Mukunda, studied why leaders fail and concluded it is grandiosity or hubris. Carol Kinsey Goman writing in her book, *The Silent Language of Leaders: How Body Language Can Help—Or Hurt How You Lead,* argues based on her research: "When first introduced to a leader, we immediately and unconsciously assess him or her for warmth and authority. The least effective leaders are those who are regarded as both cold and inept."

Bill George, a Professor of Management Practice at Harvard University and former CEO of Medtronics, wrote an article in the *Harvard Business Working Knowledge* in which he outlined how leaders lose their way, citing some notorious examples of failures of moral and ethical leadership. George goes on to argue that leaders need to devote themselves to personal development that cultivates "their inner compass which requires reframing their leadership from being heroes to being servants of the people they led". He goes on to say "when leaders focus on external gratification instead of inner satisfaction, they lose their grounding".

Psychologist and researcher Amy Brunell of Ohio State University has studied leadership and expresses concern about the prevalence of narcissism in leadership positions. Her study published in the journal *Personality and Social Psychology*, comes from a study of business managers. She says "Narcissists have an inflated view of their talents and abilities and are all about themselves," adding, "It's not surprising that narcissists become leaders. They like power. They are egotistical and they are usually charming and extraverted. The problem is they don't necessarily make better leaders."

Bill George says it this way: "One of the greatest myths of the past decade is that CEOs are primarily responsible for the success of corporations which caused us to hire the superstar at great cost and terrible results." Kevin Dutton, author of *The Wisdom of Psychopaths* argues "Traits that are common among psychopathic serial killers—a grandiose sense of self-worth, persuasiveness, superficial charm, ruthlessness, lack of remorse and the manipulation of others—are also shared by politicians and world leaders. Individuals, in other words, running not from the police, but for office. Such a profile allows those with these traits do what they like when they like, completely unfazed by the social, moral or legal consequences of their actions."

In their book, *Snakes in Suits: When Psychopaths Go To Work,* Paul Babiak and Robert Hare, argue while psychopaths may not be ideally suited for traditional work environments by virtue of a lack of desire to develop good interpersonal relationships, they have other abilities such as reading people and masterful influence and persuasion skills that can make it difficult to see them as the psychopaths they are. According to their and others' studies up to 25% of executives could be assessed as psychopaths, a much higher figure than the general population figure of 1%.

Robert Hare's Psychopathology Checklist suggests psychopathy as found in organizations has the following characteristics:

1. Social deviance and anti-social behavior (such as irresponsibility, impulsivity, unstable relationships, poor behavioral control, need for stimulation/rewards, promiscuous sexual behavior, criminal versatility and parasitic lifestyle).

2. Aggressive narcissism (superficial charm, grandiose sense of self worth, pathological lying, cunning/manipulative, lack of remorse or guilt, emotionally shallow, lack of empathy, and failure to accept personal responsibility for own actions).

Manifred Kets de Vries, a distinguished Clinical Professor of Leadership Development and Organizational Change at INSEAD has published a paper on the subject. He calls the corporate psychopath the "SOB — Seductive Operational Bully". SOBs don't usually end up in jail or psychiatric hospital but they do thrive in an organizational setting. SOBs can be found wherever power, status, or money is at stake, de Vries says. "They talk about themselves endlessly; they like to be in the limelight. In some ways they are like children, believing that they are the center of the universe, unable to recognize the needs and rights of others. They appear to be charming yet can be covertly hostile and domineering, seeing their 'victims' merely as targets and opportunities; like master and slave, they try to dominate and humiliate them. For them, the end always justifies the means. SOB executives have no qualms about buying up companies, tearing them apart, firing all the employees and selling off parts of it to earn a nice profit. 'Downsizing' comes easily to them. They are not concerned about the welfare of their employees, or about their mental health," de Vries argues.

Part of the reason why an increasing number of psychopaths have been drawn into leadership positions in the corporate world is its shift to "short termism." Organizations and indeed entire countries have increasingly focused on shorter-term results for shareholders/stakeholders, and a utilitarian view of doing whatever it takes to get succeed, no matter the cost to people and the environment.

Sydney Finkelstein, author of *Why Smart Executives Fail,* researched several spectacular failures during a six-year period. He concluded that these CEOs had similar deadly habits:

- Habit 1: They see themselves and their companies as dominating their environment. Warning sign: A lack of respect for others
- Habit 2: They identify too closely with the company, losing the boundary between personal and corporate interests. Warning sign: They define themselves by their job
- Habit 3: They think they are the only ones who have all the right answers. Warning Sign: They have few followers
- Habit 4: They ruthlessly eliminate anyone who isn't completely supportive. Warning Sign: A lot of subordinates are either fired or quit
- Habit 5: They are obsessed with photos, speeches, appearances and publications in which they represent the company. Warning Sign: They blatantly seek out media
- Habit 6: They underestimate obstacles. Warning Sign: Excessive hype and little substance
- Habit 7: They stubbornly rely on past achievements and successes. Warning sign: They consistently refer to what worked for them in the past.

David Dotlich and Peter C. Cairo, in their book, *Why CEOs Fail: The 11 Behaviors That Can Derail Your Climb To The Top And How To Manage Them,* present 11 cogent reasons why CEOs fail, most of which have to do with hubris, ego and a lack of emotional intelligence.

Carol Dueck, in her book, *Mindset,* asks, "How did CEO and gargantuan ego become synonymous? If the more self-efficacy growth-minded people are the true shepherds of industry why are so many companies out looking for the larger-than-life leaders-even when these leaders may at the end, be committed to themselves rather than to the company?"

Tomas Charmoro-Premuzic, writing in the *Harvard Business Review* blog, contends, "In the era of multimedia politics, leadership is commonly downgraded to just another form of entertainment and charisma is indispensable for keeping the audience engaged." He goes on to describe the dark side of charismatic leadership, arguing it disguises psychopaths; and fosters collective narcissism.

Here are the signs of a big ego or hubris in leaders:
- They talk incessantly about their problems
- They rely on their personal perspective of events without considering others' views
- They express an opinion when none is called for
- They judge and categorize people and events as good or bad, for or against them
- They react strongly to being questioned
- They want others to be impressed by their power, wealth or status
- They rely upon external events or financial rewards to be happy
- They are frustrated and angry when things don't go their way
- They love to be the center of attention and in the limelight
- They can be very charming and manipulative
- They take credit when things go well and assign blame when they don't
- They feel self-conscious about how they were seen or judged by others
- They seek approval of others because they liked them or because they had power over others
- They feel threatened when others disagree with them or exercised their independent judgment
- They insist on being right about something even when doing so upsets their peace of mind or the peace of mind of others
- They feel frustrated that things were not the way "they ought to be"
- They insist that there is one perfect solution to a problem while believing that only they understand that solution
- They define themselves in terms of their past accomplishments or in terms of others' shortcomings
- They focus their energy on what they were up against while finding it difficult to articulate values and principles that they stand for.

Part of the problem of leadership failure comes from our stereotype of what a leader should be. Popular culture, fed by Hollywood and the media show an image of leadership as a casting type—handsome, square jawed, white male over six feet tall with big booming voice and extraverted personality. Also, many of our ideas of leadership come from our experiences working in command-and-control or authoritarian hierarchies. These hierarchies have left huge legacies, which hamper organizations in capitalizing on collective intelligence and productivity.

Many leaders and their followers believe that they can control everything in their environment. This belief about leadership being control is pervasive in our organizations today. However, my experience as an executive coach has told me that actually controlling leaders are fearful or mistrusting of the decisions their employees might make.

When leaders rely on their ego's way of doing things—firefighting, controlling others, or coercion, they strive to win and see themselves as external objects to be manipulated. It is based on separateness. In the grip of their ego thinking, they externalize. This means they try to find an outer course for their inner state of mind. For example, when they feel thoughts of anxiety or depression, they scan the external world for an explanation of their emotional state. And they see behavior in others that really bothers them, then their ego, and their defensive brain want to project blame, criticism, judgment onto others for what really exists in themselves.

As a result, for those who aspire to leadership, the faith in superstars persists. It is a primitive belief, suitable in a time when the masses were uneducated and less able. It also allows the masses to not take responsibility for their lives, by giving it to the leader, and blaming the leader when things go wrong.

Many people who aspire to leadership are taught to see themselves separate from everyone else—special. This is a kind of false individualism. False individualists have an exaggerated belief in their own abilities and in the power of their own mind. They believe they should be in charge of shaping the environment around them, rather than allowing the environment to help inform and guide their choices. A person can barely control himself or herself, how can they aspire to control the universe?

No matter where in the world you look, there is turmoil, there is deceit and there is conflict. Power, influence and greed are the predominant driving forces in free market business today. Our business leaders are more focused on being the best in the world rather than the **best for the world**. Their egos are in need of nurturing. Old paradigm leaders lead from a place of fear — fear that they are not loved enough, fear that they are not enough period, fear that they won't be accepted, and fears about their own self worth.

In contrast, new paradigm leaders -- mindful leaders -- move beyond the fear of their egos. They are self-assured in their ability to survive. They have embraced the values that are common to every human soul. They recognize the need to find a greater meaning to their lives. They want to make a difference, they have mastered their emotions and given themselves to service to humanity.

It's clear that the storm of leadership is upon us, and we need to find leaders who can move us to the eye of the storm, to an oasis of calm so we can collectively see the way to the other side of the storm, and transform the chaos.

What's missing?

While the perspective of what motivates leaders, and what behaviors have the greatest impact has been well documented, the same can't be said for an examination of leaders from the "inside-out." That is to say, understanding what's going on inside a leader, and how that knowledge can be used to reshape leaders and leadership practices more powerfully.

The following questions about leadership still need to be answered:

1. What can neuroscience research tell us about how leaders' brains function in a variety of situations, and what can it tell us about the nature of great leaders' brains?
2. What is the nature of thinking patterns of good leaders that may be different than non-leaders?
3. What is the nature of emotional responses of good leaders that may be different than non-leaders?
4. What is the internal "story" that good leaders tell themselves about who they are?
5. How do good leaders go about the processes of self-awareness and self-mastery?
6. What is the importance and nature of reflective practices of good leaders?

The answers to these and other related questions will give us a much better picture of what constitutes mindful leadership, and will be the subject of the next few chapters.

Summary of Key Points:

- The question of what constitutes good leadership has been the subject of investigation and theorizing since ancient times
- Early theories of leadership focused on the characteristics or traits of leaders; these theories have for the most part been questioned by researchers as too simplistic, despite the still wide acceptance of this perspective by the general public
- More recent theories which describe leadership competencies also have been questioned by researchers, although they still do form the basis of many leadership development programs
- Transformational, servant, and values-based leadership theories have gained more recent credibility by leadership researchers and experts
- The inner work of leadership including self-awareness, self-mastery, thinking and emotional processes, and reflection has not received the same research attention but provides a rich field for leadership theory and practices
- Both neuroscience research and the examination of internal leadership processes can be an important component of defining what constitutes mindful leadership
- There has been a loss of public confidence in our political and business leaders
- Research points to the behavioral and personality problems of bad leaders as ego, hubris, and the need for control
- Our stereotype of the desired leader, often magnified by the media, no longer serves our society and needs to be changed
- Recruiting leaders with integrity, and avoiding the trap of selecting those based on charisma and narcissism, presents a big challenge to talent management
- Often, leaders' behavior can be characterized as mindless, without adequate self-awareness and reflection on the negative impact they may be having on people and the organization.

To get more detailed resources about leadership, and neuroscience research on the subject, go to my website: http://raywilliams.ca

6 THE INNER WORK OF LEADERSHIP

"He who knows others is wise. He who knows himself is enlightened." –
Lao Tzu

Self-Awareness And The Inner Work of Leadership

The phrase *nosce teipsum*- "know thyself"- has been an ageless theme
throughout history reflected in the writings of great thinkers such as
Socrates, Ovid, Cicero, in the sayings of the Seven Sages of Greece, in early
Christian writings, in Vedic literature, and in Taoist texts. Know thyself
threads its way through history as one of the basic beliefs in life.
Contemporary thought leaders, many of them scientists, continue to drive
home this principle, especially as new discoveries in neuroscience and
related sciences support the wisdom and power of self-awareness.
An early philosophical discussion of self-awareness is that of the English
philosopher John Locke. Locke was apparently influenced by René
Descartes' statement normally translated "I think, therefore I am."

Leadership From Without

The organizational model of leadership that has been predominate since the
end of WW I emerged from the "Cartesian-Newtonian" or materialistic
worldview, predicated on man's mastery of the environment supposedly for
the good of mankind.; and the philosophy of the manipulation of our
environment. The result has been the construction of a very narrow and
destructive concept of capitalism, which in many ways has contributed to
the degradation of our world. The current challenge of leadership is how to
demonstrate performance management and at the same time, create
purpose and meaning. A living organization without inspiration or higher
purpose does not last. Organizations must be able to move from
information to knowledge to wisdom.

The basic assumption of the "cult of performance" is based on systems thinking, particularly that field of systems thinking that assumes that human systems are cybernetic systems and it is on this assumption that policy is built. Good performance is a necessary leadership outcome and in the rational domain—financial-- easily measurable. A difficulty, however, centers on the notion of the measurement of purpose and meaning. How do you measure the non-rational, postmodern notion of spiritual leadership?

Joel Barker, author of *Paradigms: The Business of Discovering the Future,* claims that once the paradigm shifts everything goes back to zero, by which he means you are back at the starting line with the new paradigm, with no elements of the previous paradigm being present. By implication, it is fundamentally impossible to change the current organizational paradigm by fiddling with it as long as it is based on performance and economic rationalism. It's impossible because the paradigm is based on the western world view of linear growth and on self-interest, in which winning or the misinterpreted "survival of the fittest" is all that counts. The result is a deeply imbalanced world with a future of business as usual.

Business schools, management gurus and thought leaders focus on delivering an outcome in the shortest possible time that is measurable by participants which in turn determines leaders' viability and status within the business community. Bill Emmott, the editor of the *Economist,* wrote in 2004 : "The inequality of resources and power is another inherent weakness within capitalism. Indeed, one of capitalism's main motors is the very desire to create inequality, an inequality between those who succeed and those who fail. It is a competitive system. The incentive to create wealth, to build successful businesses, is an incentive to become unequal."

Robert Kegan contends that the complexity of today's work world translates into challenges very few people can meet without experiencing high levels of stress. From a developmental perspective, he mentions that what is needed to meet novel job requirements is not the introduction of new skills but rather reaching a new level of consciousness—a change in the way one gives meaning and acts in this world.

In the field of management Karl Khunert and his colleagues go even further by stating that transformational leadership is strongly associated to the leader's consciousness development. Four empirical studies show how the leaders with more advanced developed consciousness are better at convincing subordinates and superiors to consider different ways of seeing, thinking and acting. They are capable of greater collaboration and when taking action often reframe and negotiate not only their ways of seeing but also ways of collaborating. David Rooke and William Torbert observe that those higher consciousness leaders are looked on as learning leaders and participated more significantly in organizational transformations. Gervase Bushe showed that more advanced conscious leaders were better able to manage closeness and intimacy.

In a research study Paul McDonald at the University of Wellington's School of Management, argues the following:

- Self-awareness is gained through introspection and personal insight and externally through social interaction and attention to one's social impact. It is an awareness and trust in one's motives, feelings and desires and self-relevant cognitions
- It is important for leaders to avoid denial, distortion and or exaggeration and remain objective, and therefore ego defense mechanisms may compel individuals to engage in self-delusion both in terms of private self-knowledge and externally based evaluative information
- Internalized moral perspective. This incorporates self-regulation and congruence with internal values, beliefs and moral standards as opposed to external social pressures. Internal moral perspective manifests itself in the leader's consistent behavior in support of a set of internal values and standards
- It seems today more than ever business leaders have become too self-focused. While it is important for leaders to become fully self-aware and know their internal state, often what is neglected is the ability of the leader to anticipate his or her impact and influence on others.

Leaders need to use the self-knowledge they gain through reflective practices to identify and connect with their sources of strength, meaning and joy. This connection may be made by practices such as journaling , meditation, creative expression, enjoying friends and family, nature, participating in the community, developing rituals for cultivating forgiveness, gratitude, and compassion, transforming leadership tasks into caring-healing interactions and demonstrating a willingness to explore one's own beliefs, feelings and values for self growth.

Many of our ideas about leadership arise from our experiences working in command-and-control hierarchies. Such hierarchies have left huge legacies — all around us we see firms failing to capitalize on their organizational intelligence and losing their competitiveness.

The emotionally immature hold a false view of leadership. They associate leadership with the privileges and powers they would wield were they to become leaders — dream of staff standing by to carry out their every whim; dream of a large salary; dream of people being intimidated by them as they walk the halls. How different is that from the expectations of European kings or ancient Roman emperors?

The belief that external circumstances cause our troubles is almost universally held; the world seems to be the cause of our thoughts, feelings and behavior. But this is mistaken. When we stop blaming, we stop making up stories about the external world.

When we rely on our ego's way of doing things --- firefighting, controlling others, and coercion, we strive to win and see ourselves as external objects to be manipulated and therefore seeing the whole and connections to others are denied.

Physicists have now demolished the view we once had that the universe sits safely "out there," that we can observe that goes on in it from behind a foot thick slab of plate glass without ourselves being involved with what goes on. The reality is we are not the observer, but the participator.

In the grip of our ego thinking we externalize. To externalize means we try to find an outer cause for our inner state of mind. For example, when we feel thoughts of anxiety or depression, we scan the external world for an explanation of our emotional state. Our ego loves to provide external explanations such as "I am anxious because I've heard the news", or "I'm anxious what may happen to…" And when we see behavior in others that really bothers us, our ego, our defensive and protective brain, wants to project blame, criticism, judgment onto the other person for what really exists in ourselves. The reality is that external conditions are not a cause for our inner condition.

When we search for a cause outside of ourselves for how we are feeling and behaving, we are always wrong. The truth is we create a feeling inside ourselves first; then we search for an outside cause. This allows us to escape responsibility for our choice to value our ego-generated thoughts.

Great leaders take complete responsibility for the emotions they experience. It is unworthy of a leader to attribute emotions to external situations. We are not responsible for what others are doing, but we are responsible for how we experience what others are doing. We see the world not as it is, but as we are.

Why Self-Awareness Is So Important For Leaders

Dee Hock, the founder of Visa, says "the first and paramount responsibility of anyone who purports to manage is to manage self: One's own integrity character, ethics, knowledge, wisdom, temperament, words and acts. Without management of self, no one is fit for leadership."

A study conducted in 2010 by Green Peak Partners and Cornell's School of Industrial and Labor Relations examined 72 executives' interpersonal traits at public and private companies with revenues from $50 million to $5 billion. The study included in part this conclusion: 'Leadership searches give short shrift to 'self-awareness,' which should actually be a top criterion. Interestingly, a high self-awareness score was the strongest predictor of overall success.

This is not altogether surprising as executives who are aware of their weaknesses are often better able to hire subordinates who perform well in categories in which the leader lacks acumen. These leaders are also more able to entertain the idea that someone on their team may have an idea that is even better than their own. The qualities commonly associated with leadership – being authoritative, decisive, forceful, perhaps somewhat controlling – if not moderated by a high degree of awareness as to how one comes across and is perceived by others, are also qualities that have the potential to easily alienate those on the receiving end.

Over the years I've seen numerous executive careers derailed by lack of self-awareness. Individuals felt they were omnipotent and took crazy risks, or didn't recognize when actions that felt authoritative were actually demoralizing, or in general didn't have an accurate "read" on how others were decoding the messages they were sending.

New research by Korn Ferry analysts David Zes and Dana Landis provides a large body of data for the first time regarding the direct relationship between leader self-awareness and organizational financial performance. Zes and Landis write in their whitepaper, "A Better Return on Self-Awareness," that "public companies with a higher rate of return (ROR) also employ professionals who exhibit higher levels of self-awareness."

This research with its hard evidence makes it impossible to cast self-awareness aside as a soft skill any longer. Self-awareness is the most crucial developmental breakthrough for accelerating personal leadership growth and authenticity. Learning to pause to build self-awareness is an evolving process critical to leader success. It is extremely valuable to know ourselves in order to leverage our potentialities:

- We need to know our strengths to assert them in the appropriate circumstances
- We need to know our vulnerabilities, weaknesses, and distressing emotions, to check them and to prevent asserting them inappropriately and in non-value creating ways
- When we are not self-aware, people around us have a better sense of our strengths and weaknesses than we do, and we lose credibility
- When we are self-aware, we are more in touch with reality; people trust and respect us more.

Power and Empathy
Being able to see, understand and deal effectively with others' perspectives is key to successful leadership (as well as personal life). That capacity, part of self-awareness, is empathy. Two recent studies show its crucial role. One looked at the impact of power in an organization upon behavior; the other, its impact upon brain activity. Both studies found that increased power reduces empathy.

One study, conducted by Adam D. Galinsky and colleagues at Northwestern's Kellogg School of Management, found that increased power tends to make one more self-centered and self-assured, but not in a good way. The researchers found that power makes one "prone to dismiss or, at the very least, misunderstand the viewpoints of those who lack authority."

High-power individuals "anchor too heavily on their own perspectives and demonstrate a diminished ability to correctly perceive others' perspectives," according to Galinsky and his team, adding that: "As power increases, power-holders are more likely to assume that others' insights match their own."

Another study by Canadian researchers, found the same thing by looking at brain activity when people have power. They found that increased power diminishes the ability to be empathic and compassionate because power appears to affect the "mirror system" of the brain, through which one is "wired" to experience what another person is experiencing. Researchers found that even the smallest bit of power shuts down that part of the brain and the ability to empathize with others.

These are highly important findings, because empathy, compassion and overall self-awareness are qualities of a developed, mature mind one that's resilient to stress, able to manage internal conflicts, experience interconnection with others, and maintains personal well-being. Emotionally detached, un-empathic persons, unaware of their personal motives or truths are not going to be very effective as a CEO or senior leader. We see examples of the consequences from time-to-time, when a CEO resigns or is fired.

Building Self-Awareness
Self-awareness builds from honest self-appraisal about emotional strengths and vulnerabilities; your values and attitudes; personality traits; and unresolved conflicts.

One of Google's earliest executives, <u>Chade-Meng Tan, teaches a popular course</u> for Google employees that helps build such qualities. The program has demonstrated positive benefits for success and well-being. Scott Keller, a director at McKinsey & Company, described the importance of overcoming self-interest and delusion in the *Harvard Business Review*. He emphasizes the need for openness to personal growth and development, because "deep down, (leaders) do not believe that it is they who need to change..." and that "the real bottleneck...is knowing what to change at a personal level."

A survey of 75 members of the Stanford Graduate School of Business Advisory Council rated self-awareness as the most important capability for leaders to develop. Executives need to know where their natural inclinations lie in order to boost them or compensate for them. Self-awareness is about identifying personal idiosyncrasies — the characteristics that executives take to be the norm but actually represent the exception.

Sometimes self-awareness comes early in one's career, prompted by a comment from a trusted colleague or boss. In an article in *Fortune International*, Lauren Zalaznick, now chairman, Entertainment & Digital Networks and Integrated Media for NBC-Universal, recalled that the best advice she ever received was from her first boss, who told her: "Throughout your career, you're going to hear lots of feedback from show-makers and peers and employees and bosses. If you hear a certain piece of feedback consistently and you don't agree with it, it doesn't matter what you think. Truth is, you're being perceived that way."

In observing leaders for 40 years, I have never seen someone fail for lack of IQ. But I have seen hundreds fail who lacked emotional intelligence and self-awareness. Psychologist Daniel Goleman first popularized the concept in his 1995 book, *Emotional Intelligence*. He defined EQ as competencies driving leadership performance, including: Self-awareness or reading emotions and recognizing their impact; self-management or controlling emotions and adapting to change; social awareness or understanding others' emotions and comprehending social networks; and relationship management; or inspiring, influencing, and developing others while managing conflict.

Another study included 435 executive leaders and more than 5000 contributing team members, comprised of the leaders' managers, peers, and direct reports. Organizations within the continental United States, with most of the participants coming from financial, engineering, and manufacturing institutions employed all participants. Most leaders oversaw a team of at least five or more direct reports and had an average annual income of over $100,000, indicating these are middle to senior level leaders with a history of leadership experience.

While all competencies measured were found to be important in leadership effectiveness the strongest correlation was found between self-awareness and leadership effectiveness. These findings demonstrate that while behaviors associated with competencies such as being adaptable and accountable are important in being an effective leader, they are less important than the behaviors associated with the competency of self-awareness. Leaders judged to have high levels of self-awareness/self-management are also the leaders judged to be models of effective leadership who can produce superior results on a consistent basis. Leaders with low levels of self- awareness/self-management are the leaders judged to be poor models of leadership and cannot consistently produce superior results.

The results of this study suggest that self-awareness is one of the most critical competencies to be developed in order to have the greatest impact on creating greater leadership effectiveness.

Christopher Edgar, the author of the book, *Inner Productivity: A Mindful Path to efficiency and Enjoyment in Your Work,* says "inner productivity is the mental and emotional state that allows you to get the most done and find the most enjoyment in your work." Inner productivity is "about becoming aware of and transforming the way you think and feel about what you do." We have so much mental and mental "clutter" that interferes with our motivation and focus. Before we reach for simple external solutions such as time management techniques or office and file organizers and calendar organizers, we need to bring order to our inner experience — thoughts, emotions and sensations that come up as you engage in work. Then we need to focus on feeling more focused and motivated and joyful about our work.

Paying attention to our inner experience runs counter to our beliefs in Western culture, which is that we should ignore or push away the thoughts and sensations that come up while we're working and "deal with them" on "our own time". And we're not only expected to repress our so-called negative emotions and thoughts in our culture, we're also supposed to hold back our passion for what we do, the happiness and joy. It's considered unusual today for someone to say they love their job.

Very few business writers and management consultants or experts today examine our inner experience of working. They assume the only way to transform our inner experience is to change from the outside in — altering our external environment.

So much of our beliefs about ignoring out internal state come from childhood and our desire to make children grow up too soon. In effect, children are taught to distort or repress their feelings. So often we hear these phrases: "stop crying", "that's enough now", "be nice to your sister", "how many times have I told you to [fill in the reason]".

In a similar way, we are taught that work is not meant to inspire us, fill us with passion or joy, but rather work is a thing to do until we can get on with the really important things in our life—hobbies, fun activities, vacations, etc.

So when you hear someone say, "I'm following my bliss," in reference to work or their job, we see them as being weak, selfish, childish, or "acting like a child." If we want to act like adults, we must keep or chin up, bear the boring or dismal work and suffer. Given this mindset, it's no small wonder we see the typical worker as being emotionless and work as boring.

Unfortunately, much productivity advice urges us to fight against our inner experience, giving us pointers like "force yourself to do the toughest task first" ,"tell that lazy part of you to shut up" ,"kick your fear in the rear", or become your own drill sergeant. This attitude encourages us to be self-critical rather than treating ourselves with compassion. We flee from our emotions when we turn our attention to something else to take our minds off what we're feeling.

We may feel that we are "saving time," when we push away our inner experience as we work—that letting ourselves feel emotion would draw our attention away from the task we're trying to do. But the reverse is true. The very things we do to escape from our inner experience also prevents us from getting our work done. So fighting or fleeing our thoughts and emotions actually wastes time instead of saving it.

A more serious effect occurs when we try to avoid or block or push away thoughts and feelings—if we keep them at bay long enough they become monsters, and start sabotaging our efforts to accomplished our goals. An example is someone who represses anger for long periods of time, and then has an explosive episode at work directed at a work colleague or boss.

In fact, most thoughts and emotions we experience ultimately pass — within minutes or seconds—when we stop running away from or shutting them off. Then, when the thoughts and feelings have naturally passed, we can gently return our attention to our work, without the need to punish, convince or coax ourselves into getting back on task. This approach of relating to our inner experiences at work is acceptance, and it consumes far less time and energy than fighting or fleeing from our thoughts and feelings. The result is an increase in our productivity.

Another advantage of learning to be with our thoughts and sensations, as opposed to running from or blocking them, is that it helps us assume more and more control over how we live our lives, particularly if we're constantly fighting or fleeing our emotional state, there's a sense in which we aren't really in control of our behavior.

Being self-aware means we learn how to intentionally respond to experiences in our life instead of reacting to them. Accepting our inner experience as a way to show ourselves genuine self-compassion which means accepting all of our experiences without calling them inappropriate and trying to escape from them.

Accepting or allowing what you are experiencing doesn't mean grudgingly resigning yourself to it. That's the same as fighting against your experience and is passive-aggressive behavior. Nor do you need to pretend to be happy about what you're experiencing to accept it—you don't need to force yourself to smile when you're feeling down. Accepting your inner experience is more a matter of removing the labels you put on it. Rather than treating the thoughts and sensations you have as "bad" or problems to be fixed, or trying to convince yourself when you feel wonderful when you don't ; see if you can let them be, just as they are, without mentally judging or categorizing them. Without the mental labels "boring", "bad", etc. In doing so, you can reduce the intensity and pain of negative feelings.

You can also achieve a sense of ease and inspiration in your work by seeing thoughts and feelings that come up to be there, but also as a source of valuable inner wisdom. Whatever enters your consciousness as you work—fear, despair, fretting or angry—it likely has something to teach you about where you have room to grow as human beings. This is an inside-out process--how you feel, interpret, process these situations and decide on your response.

The Inside-Out Perspective

Kevin Cashman in his book Leadership *From The Inside Out: Becoming A Leader for Life,* talks about this intersection of inside-out as it applies to leaders. On the one hand, the leaders' environment obviously affects what goes on in the leaders' mind and, in return, the leaders' mental processing generates responses and actions that impact their environment. External and internal, it is a dynamic whole. You cannot seriously consider leadership development without addressing both elements. Cashman says that typical leadership development programs in organizations concentrate almost exclusively on the "outside", the *doing* part: leadership actions, behaviors, competencies, techniques, and so forth. For this reason he has chosen to focus on the "inside" or *being* part: how you go about continually growing your inner self as a leader.

Neuroscience and Leadership

Many researchers who recognize the need to go beyond traditional leadership assessment methods, which typically involve evaluating leader behaviors and qualities through some sort of survey process through which followers or peers rate a leader's effectiveness have recently questioned the efficacy of traditional leadership development methods.

We have studied leaders' personality, intelligence, values, attitudes and even behavior. But seldom has anyone ventured physiologically inside of leaders. Advances in fMRI (functional magnetic resonance imaging), machines, have generated greater interest in more holistic approaches to studying leadership are giving us a whole new picture.

Research in the realm of cognitive neuroscience can offer some insight into how the brain might support leaders in their emotional connections with followers. Specifically, certain things that leaders do — namely, influencing others' moods, understanding the emotions of the self and others, and making decisions regarding how to use emotions to influence and inspire others, reflect a competency typically referred to as emotional intelligence. Drawing upon individual differences in the areas of the brain associated with emotional expressiveness, empathy, and emotional regulation, researchers have suggested that emotionally intelligent behavior has a neurological basis.

Leaders need to build relationships that inspire and motivate others to do their best, innovate and adapt. In *Primal Leadership* by Daniel Goleman, Richard Boyatzis & Annie McKee, and *Resonant Leadership* by Boyatzis & Anne McKee, they synthesize a great deal of research to support the idea that effective leaders build resonant relationships with those around them. At the same time, the authors argue that less effective leaders or those that are more one-sided seem to create dissonant relationships.

The authors used a neuroscience research methodology, the fMRI to study the neural mechanisms that took place in the brains of resonant, high quality relationship leaders. Middle-aged subjects were asked about critical incidents with leaders in their experiences. FMRI scans were conducted, with cues developed from these experiences. The researchers reported that recalling specific experiences with resonant leaders significantly activated fourteen regions of interest in the brain, while dissonant leaders activated six and deactivated eleven regions. Experiences with resonant leaders activated neural systems involved in arousing attention, the social or default, mirror system, and other regions associated with approach relationships.

Meanwhile, dissonant leaders deactivated systems involved in social or default networks, the mirror system, activated those regions associated with narrowing attention and those associated with less compassion and more negative emotions.

The authors concluded that dissonant leaders seem to turn people off, alienate them, and damage others' motivation. The emerging neuroscience findings suggest a basic reason why inspiring and supportive relationships are important. The authors contend they help activate openness to new ideas and a more social orientation to others.

These insights may change the focus of a leader's actions away from a results-orientation toward a relationship orientation, they argue. This does not preclude the concern with results, but could show why being first and foremost concerned about one's relationships may then enable others to perform better and more innovatively – and lead to better results.

The Leader's Emotional Brain
Effective leadership involves the regulation of one's own emotions. Furthermore, it involves an understanding of and an ability to influence the positive emotions of others despite the ambiguity, setbacks, or fears that they might otherwise face.

Using the terminology of emotional intelligence, balance is achieved by promoting the positive emotions associated with optimism and excitement, while keeping more disruptive negative emotions such as anxiety, selfishness, fear, anger and sadness, in check.

Various authors have proposed a specific neurological basis for emotional intelligence or skills. Goleman and his colleagues noted that emotional intelligence has a basis in brain circuitry and further suggested that it derives from how cortical regions of the brain interpret and manage neurotransmitter signals from the brain's limbic system.

Certain parts of the brain may help a person to balance emotions in decision-making, especially in situations in which outcomes are ambiguous or uncertain. There is also recent research showing that regions of the cortex may help to assess risk and guide behaviors in anticipation of emotional consequences, including such negative consequences as fear and despair.

The frontal parts of the brain may be especially involved in the regulation and expression of emotions, as well as higher cognitive functioning such as goal-directed or visionary behavior. For instance, researchers found the right frontal part of the brain to be essential for effective interpersonal communication and social relationships. Moreover, it has been shown that right frontal dysfunction gives rise to antisocial behavior and an inability to understand relationships with other people (i.e., social skills, mood control, and awareness of self) and difficulties balancing emotions in decision making under conditions of uncertainty.

Rethinking Emotional Regulation

We've long known that stress affects performance. Studies by Matt Lieberman show that the brain has just one main "braking system," sitting behind the left and right temple, which is used for all types of braking -- mental, physical and emotional.

Studies show that the braking system is activated when one labels an emotion in simple words. Yet, in our culture, people prefer not to talk about emotions, and tend to suppress them instead. But suppressing an emotional expression backfires, making the emotion more intense, affecting memory and creating a threat response in others. In short, our intuitive strategies for regulating emotions (not talking about them) do exactly the opposite of what we intend, leaving us less capable of dealing with the world adaptively. Leaders, who deal with intense emotions all day, could do well to develop emotional regulation techniques that truly keep them cool under pressure.

Leadership researchers have suggested that leaders' emotions may influence followers in ways that impact leadership effectiveness. Specifically, research on leader positive emotion and affect suggests that leader emotional displays may influence followers either by motivating them because they convey positivity, or because they are contagious and engender positive emotions in followers that guide their behavior.

Research shows that displays of leader positive emotions were associated with high ratings of charismatic leadership and more positive affect in followers. Similarly, expressions of positivity by leaders led to higher ratings of transformational leadership. A yet unanswered question in this arena is whether such leaders are predisposed to the aforementioned emotional behavior and whether such capacities can be developed. Preliminary evidence suggests that the brains of optimistic leaders may indeed be different.

Other research has suggested that negative emotions are stronger than positive emotions. Dr. Rick Hanson sees it as two metaphors. Negative emotions pass through our brains and stick like "Velcro" and positive emotions pass through our brains and pass through like "Teflon." As a result, we would suspect that the contagion of negative emotions would ignite a stronger neural sequence than positive emotions. This may serve evolutionary functions, but, paradoxically, it may limit learning. Arousal of strong negative emotions stimulates the Sympathetic Nervous System(SNS), which inhibits access to existing neural circuits and involves cognitive emotional and perceptual impairment. A contagion of positive emotions seems to arouse the Parasympathetic Nervous System (PNS), which stimulates adult neurogenesis (growth of new neurons), a sense of well-being, better immune system functioning and cognitive, and emotional and perceptual openness.

The sustainability of leadership effectiveness is directly a function of a person's ability to adapt and achieve neural plasticity. The SNS and PNS are both needed for human functioning. They each have an impact on neural plasticity. Arousal affects the growth of the size and shape of our brain. Neurogenesis allows the human to build new neurons. The endocrines aroused in the PNS allow the immune system to function at its best to help preserve existing tissue.

The most likely implication of these results is that leaders bear the primary responsibility for knowing what they are feeling and therefore, managing the contagion that they infect in others. It requires a heightened emotional self-awareness. This means having techniques to notice the feelings; label or understand what they are; and then signal yourself that you should do something to change your mood and state. Merely saying to yourself that you will "put on a happy face" or "keep your chin up," does not hide the fact they you are unconsciously transmitting your real feelings to others around you.

Leaders are infecting others around them with specific feelings. Some of those feelings help them to perform better and innovate and some are debilitating and inhibit adaptive thinking. Remember, negative feelings, even the unconscious ones, will easily overwhelm positive ones. Leaders, because of their position of power, have a greater affect on others in a social or work environment. Being able to change their internal state might be one of the most powerful techniques they can learn in becoming an effective leader—one who inspires others to learn adapt and perform at their best.

Leaders should reshape their jobs to become coaches in helping to motivate and inspire those around them. But not just any form of coaching will help. Coaching others with compassion appears to activate neural systems that help a person open themselves to new possibilities—to learn and adapt. Meanwhile, the more typical coaching of others to change in imposed ways (trying to get them to conform to the views of the boss) puts the person in a defensive posture.

The Brain and Compassion and Empathy

Brain research has pinpointed an area of the brain associated with perspective taking. For example, results of neuroimaging and fMRI studies have found clear activation in certain areas of the cortex when taking another's perspective (i.e., putting oneself in the shoes of another). There is also strong evidence from fMRI studies, as well as from lesion studies in neurological patients, which suggest that patients with brain injuries in the areas associated with emotional processing are not able to distinguish their own perspective from others. Overall, there appears to be a neurological explanation for why some individuals are better at understanding the feelings, emotions, and reactions of followers.

In addition to empathizing with the emotions of followers, effective leaders also need to regulate and control their own emotions for a variety of reasons. For example, leaders may need to suppress negative emotions in certain situations such as anger toward a follower in order to avoid unhealthy conflict or confrontation. On the other hand, a leader may need to suppress positive emotions, such as liking or attraction toward specific followers, to avoid claims of favoritism. Other examples include the leader needing to offer or praise to motivate followers, or to be particularly calm during times of crisis. Although emotion regulation can carry some negative consequences due to emotional labor, it is generally considered to be an adaptive behavior to leader–follower communication.

Building trust as a leader

Our brains make a determination of the trustworthiness of people within milliseconds of meeting them. This initial evaluation continues to be updated as more information is obtained and processed. The brain simultaneously is evaluating physical appearance, gestures, voice tone, the content of spoken communication, and many other factors. All of this is happening so quickly that most people will find it difficult to express exactly why they trust or distrust a person. So how does a leader build trust?

Here are a few suggestions based on how our brains process information:

- Make people feel safe. Our brains place top priority on survival, so anyone who demonstrates that they can reduce or eliminate threats to others' survival is deemed trustworthy. Remember that in today's world, threats could mean a challenge to our physical survival, but also could mean a danger to our prestige, income, or comfort or psychological and emotional well-being
- Demonstrate fairness. Studies have shown that human beings may be hard-wired for fairness as an evolutionary development. People who perceive that they have been treated unfairly will quickly move to a state of distrust
- Think about how you appear to others. When we watch someone else, our brains are activated in the same way that the brain of the person we are observing is activated—through the function of special "mirror neurons." This means that you might unintentionally transfer your own feelings of distrust to others. The trick is that you can't fake trust; our brains can tell the difference. You actually must believe that your co-workers are trustworthy to transmit this signal to them. In turn, their brains will start feeling trust towards you as a result.

At the *Universiti Sains Malaysia*, researchers are studying "neuroleadership" from the perspective of transformational leadership based on the work of Bass and Burns. Where transactional leadership focuses on exchanges, which motivate followers by providing rewards and benefits for productivity, transformational leaders make decisions based on cognitive rewards, provide a climate of trust and draw out followers' higher order needs to perform beyond expectations. Transformational leaders inspire their followers to make decisions that transcend self-interest.

Motivation and the brain

Our drive to take action, achieve goals and exert effort emanates from some of our deepest and oldest brain regions. Motivation is a survival necessity, so the neural circuitry developed for it is both extensive and heavily interconnected.

You probably consider motivation a matter of conscious choice: whether you will go out for dinner tonight with friends or stay home alone and watch a movie. In the brain, decision-making, planning and control are predominantly "top-down" processes (that is, guided by conscious prefrontal cortical activity) and with this comes responsibility or seemingly simple choices like these are influenced by subconscious needs, priming and expectations. In his book, *Social: Why Our Brains Are Wired To Connect*, neuroscientist Matthew Lieberman shows that social rejection is just like physical pain. He explains the human brain is hardwired to seek interaction with other people, and that those connections are at least as important as human sunlight or food, water and shelter. His research also shows that the human brain has an innate ability to consider what's important to other people, which is completely distinct from our system of thinking and reasoning.

Leaders play a crucial role in creating environments that foster threat and/or reward. There are direct implications on the performance of individuals and teams exposed to these environments. In a state of threat, the significantly stronger forces of the limbic system thinking processes effectively shut down the prefrontal cortex. This subconscious brain region bases thinking on automatic patterns that have been 'tried and true', as well as self-preservation in the face of the perceived threat. As a result, performance is driven by fear or anxiety, inducing the stress state (in turn releasing the stress chemical cortisol), which was earlier shown to compromise performance outcomes.

When employees work with a leader who promotes reward states, the opposite psychological and physiological effects occur. The prefrontal cortex is active and integrates positively with the limbic system. The reward chemical dopamine is released into the central nervous system in response to engagement in a challenging but supportive environment, and optimal performance can be achieved.

It is through the influence they have on others that leaders are seen to be in a position of power. Leaders can unleash optimal performance in their employees when they exert this power in ways that inspire and support, rather than threaten and demoralize, their teams.

Neuroscientists David Rock and Jeffrey Schwartz have argued that neuroscience has identified the building blocks needed for successful change, the most important of which is to establish undivided attention. The portion of the brain dedicated to learning and comprehension, the prefrontal cortex, requires concentration to process new information. Most people have the mental capacity to focus on only one new idea at a time. The second step is creating a vision of a positive future. People's mental maps play a central role in their perception of the world. To facilitate change, leaders must encourage moments of insight that allow people to change their maps. The brain undergoes a complex set of new neural connections. Finally leaders must find ways to keep people's attention focused on the change. It's not enough to introduce a vision once and expect others to internalize it.

Advances in neuroscience are expanding our understanding of behavior and learning. The challenge in integrating neuroscience with management behavior such as inspirational leadership include problems in attempting to build theory that would conceptually link brain activity to leadership behavior, and the use of effective technologies to measure.

The Failure Of Leadership Development Programs

Organizations invest billions annually on leadership development. Training and development programs almost universally focus in a factory-like way on inputs and outputs — absorb curriculum, check a box; learn a skill, advance a rung; submit to assessment; or fix a problem. Likewise, they leave too many people behind with an elite selection process that fast-tracks favored candidates and essentially discards the rest. They leave most people uninspired and with flavor of the month remedies, which produce little more than a grim legacy of fat binders gathering dust on shelves. Or the initial excitement of the seminar or retreat quickly fades after a short time back to "normal" at the office.

Part of the reason why leadership development programs fails is inextricably tied to our notions of what makes a good leader. Tasha Eurich, author of Bankable Leadership: *Happy People, Bottom Line Results and the Power to Deliver Both*, argues: "Though scientists spent most of the 19th century convinced that good leadership was inborn and fixed, the research of the early 20th century told a different story—that leadership is largely made."

A recent study by Richard Arvey at Singapore's NUS Business School revealed that up to 70 % of leadership is learned. But business leaders are divided. The Center for Creative Leadership reports that 20 % of C-level executives believe that leadership is born, and more than 28 % believe it's equally born and made. But, the evidence shows otherwise.

According to an MIT study, investment in leadership education and development approached $50 billion in the U.S. alone in the year 2000, and it has grown considerably since. Leadership training has become a big business, with publishers, universities and consultants jockeying to position themselves as the "go-to" partners and gurus to develop leaders. Despite these massive efforts, the picture of failed leadership persists, from the halls of government to the next startup. In particular, the track record of success for CEOs is not pretty. Research shows that most development programs fail to deliver expected returns.

The MIT study of dozens of companies over two decades identifies three "pathologies" that may account for leadership failures. The first is "the ownership is power mind-set." Older ways of managing, predominantly a command and control style persist, and these ways collide with the new realities of what makes organizations and their employees behave, which requires a system of shared accountability and responsibility. The MIT study argues that ownership and control is the wrong issue and illustrates old-world thinking. Leaving responsibility solely to the CEO or management team or HR for developing leaders is not realistic and is not successful.

The second pathology identified in the MIT study is the "productization of leadership development", or in other words, leadership development is linked to the products of the organization, rather than the overarching problems that need to be solved. This often leads to quick fixes. It is frequently seen as a leadership program based on a best-selling book or off-the-shelf leadership program purchased from a consultant. The result frequently ends up in the flavor of the month approach to training programs, which are often frequently forgotten in a short time. During tough economic times, top executives decide to curtail investments in leadership development, ushering in the return of a more Darwinian model of leadership — "the cream will rise to the top". Employees then become cynical about the company's dedication to leadership development. High-potentials hesitate before investing their energy in developmental initiatives; some of the best walk away from the organization, and others do not reach their potential for lack of strong developmental experiences. In this scenario, there are no winners.

The third pathology that the MIT study identifies is "make believe metrics". Most organizations require accountability for their expenditures, which is often driven by metrics. Today there are scorecards for virtually everything, including leadership development. However, the MIT study concludes, the use of metrics for the effectiveness of leadership development is leading them astray. Most metrics don't measure the soft skills, or strategic thinking or collaborative behavior, all of which are essential for leadership success.

Organizations tend to measure the things that are easy to measure. "The philosophy that dominates so many company cultures today is that initiatives that cannot be measured have no value. In most instances, that is a reasonable assumption. But it does not apply to leadership development — not, at least, in the quantifiable terms that dictate assessments of capital expenditures," the authors of the MIT study conclude.

Two Illustrative Cases Studies
I've had at least two experiences in coaching senior executives in large organizations in which the issue of the inner work of leadership was clearly evident—or should I say absent. In the first example, I was asked to come into work with a senior professional leader who had a worldwide reputation for his knowledge and expertise, through his research. And yet, while he was widely respected for his technical advice and published papers he had significant relationship problems with his colleagues and some of his clients. As I continued to meet with him over a period of months, it became apparent that he lacked any self-awareness, lacked the ability to regulate his emotions, and was unaware of the impact he had on others. He viewed his experience as one that was entirely external—that is, situations and people were responsible for his negative emotions and judgmental perspectives of others. While he made some progress in addressing his lack of self-awareness, his willingness to take that inner journey was not made with great gusto, and he continues to struggle with self-mastery, relying on decades of habitual behavior.

In the second experience I had coaching CEO who also was not prepared to take the inner journey of leadership, his problems revolved around his insistence that dealing with his emotional state was of no consequence, because he believed naively that he made all decisions based solely on logic and rationality. Slowly, and to his credit, he became more open to the knowledge that emotions are drivers for decisions and behaviors, and that he needed to master those as much as the next strategic plan. He took the first steps in the inner journey of leadership.

What I find interesting and somewhat amazing, is that both of these leaders in the situations I described had a successful career and risen to the top of their field based primarily on their orientation to the external world, which is a reflection of part of the problem of who we choose as leaders and their impact on organizations.

What If?

What if instead of stuffing people with curricula models and competencies, we focused on deepening their sense of purpose, expanded their ability to navigate difficult and complex times and enriched their emotional lives? What if, instead of trying to fix people, we assumed they were already full of potential and we created an environment that promoted their long-term well-being? What if we cultivated a successful inner life as front and center?

If you want to transform an organization it's not about changing systems and processes so much as it's about changing the hearts and minds of people. Developing people is a process not an event. People don't grow from the neck up. They grow from the heart not just the head.

Summary of Key Points:

- The most critical element of developing good leaders is that of self-awareness
- Leadership in the past has excessively focused on the external world and "doing things"
- The prevailing system of capitalism and business has reinforced a limited view of leadership
- Good leadership is an "inside-out" process, an internal journey
- Neuroscience research has been able to identify the connection between inspiring and "relational" leaders and certain kinds of brain activity
- Emotional regulation is one of the keys to mindful leadership behavior
- The capacity for empathy and compassion is a key leadership characteristic.

To get more resources on the inner journey of leaders, reflective leadership and the implications from neuroscience, go to my website: http://raywilliams.ca

7 MINDFUL LEADERSHIP

Regular practices of mindfulness give leaders a different perspective on their world, opening them up to ways of being which are both more focused on what matters and more observant and appreciative of what is there. Paradoxically, becoming more present enables leaders to see reality more clearly and act more purposefully and with less of their own stuff getting in the way. This is one of a number of paradoxes which we often see operating in mindful leadership: to open up for change, it is necessary to sometimes stop striving to change things; to empower others, stop talking and listen from a different place; to go forward effectively, notice the present; to achieve things, stop doing and start being.

The ratio of investing in Mindfulness training has been found to be 1 to 2.5-5.0 according to a study by Tage Sondersgaard Kristensen of Corporate Based Mindfulness Training IF Insurance, based in the Netherlands. He observed a 19% decrease in stress, 37% increase in productivity, 40% increase in focus, 34% increase in emotional control and 37% decrease in overwhelm. Stephanie Tate's study with a Fortune 500 knowledge workforce found participants in 6-9 week mindfulness course experience a 42% stress reduction, improvement in productivity, time management and job satisfaction.

Studies have documented that regular mindfulness practice elicits better attentional capabilities and more positive emotional states, mediated through neuroplastic changes in key parts of the brain involved in cognitive and emotional functioning. Mindfulness changes our intentions (making us better at self-regulation and more compassionate toward self and others); changes our attentional capacities enabling us to sustain attention for longer; switches attention more deftly when needed and inhibits unnecessary secondary processing; and finally mindfulness enhances positive emotions.

A substantial group of researchers have focused on the attentional benefits of mindfulness practices. Many of us find it hard to focus our attention on one thing. For example in a typical meeting, our minds are thinking about lunch and the weekend and whether that remark 10 minutes ago by the CEO should be taken personally, despite our efforts to focus on an issue being discussed.

Mindfulness trains people to increase their capacity to pay attention (beyond the 3-7 seconds that is normal) and to develop different qualities of attention for different situations. The capacity to give different qualities of attention to different aspects of context is highly relevant for leaders who often face multiple competing demands on their attention. What often occurs in response are patterns of "hypervigilance", giving everything a high level of suspicious attention and patterns of distraction, moving between many different issues of varying importance. In their research on the costs of multitasking, David Dean and Andrew Webb found that such habits of having poor quality attention on multiple issues simultaneously reduces efficiency not enhances it. They also note that while multitasking is an often lionized norm in workplaces, it reduces job satisfaction, feelings of health and well-being, while increasing feelings of stress and anxiety (despite or perhaps because it is addictive), and it results in lower productivity.

A range of other studies focus on the emotional benefits of regular mindfulness practice. For example, mindfulness changed habits of stress attribution, improving coping and emotional well-being. Other researchers have been particularly interested in the quality of cognitive processing such as capacities to take perspective, embrace unexpected data and make ethical decisions. For some of these psychological researchers, mindfulness is seen as a metacognitive skill involving thinking about one's habits of thinking. In two separate but related studies, these researchers found that low mindfulness was associated with the presence of self-serving cognitive justifications, self-deception and unconscious biases, in turn supporting unethical conduct such as cheating. In contrast were those who rated high on mindfulness and were more likely to uphold ethical standards and adopt a principled approach to decision-making .

Finally, a group of researchers, many of whom are part of the positive psychology movement, have documented the ways in which mindfulness mediates feelings of happiness, gratitude, joy and compassion for others. These studies generally show a correlation between mindful practices and feelings of personal well-being, the capacity to manage stress and to have a positive, appreciative outlook on life which is less subject to the ups and downs of events.

Leaders are facing what seem to be increased pressures to do more with fewer resources. They have heavy workloads and are sometimes charged with letting go of good people or making other difficult decisions. Many feel they are on the edge, close to breaking. They can't see another way forward though they may fantasize about escape. Sometimes their personal relationships are under intense strain. Relations with family and friends, as well as health, are often the casualties of the cult of workaholism.

Leaders lose sight of the pleasure and satisfaction they may have gained from work, instead feeling ground down. When we explore some of the pressures they are under, and some of these effects, their first response can be "But that's just leadership isn't it? That's the job?"

Among the reasons why many of these leaders seem to find mindfulness useful is that they can, very directly in a workshop setting or even better, over a couple of days, get an experience of being quieter and stiller, despite the chaos. Even briefly, this experience of observing their thoughts about the situation rather than being captured in them, opens up an option that wasn't there before: that they can choose their reaction. Seemingly simple but also profound, in the short term there may be no change to what's happening to us or around us. Mindfulness simply allows us to be with those happenings in a less reactive way.

Associated with mindfulness and its reduced reactivity, is the possibility of letting go of some things. Many leaders carry around in their heads ideas like "I can't let them down" or "it's my job to do those difficult things". Frequently these are punitive ideas or beliefs, which are actually not functional or useful any more. In letting go of them, leaders often find they are of more use to the people around them because their interactions are not overshadowed by these "shoulds".

A beautiful quality that sometimes unfolds with groups of leaders experimenting with mindfulness is appreciativeness. Whether it's in newly formed groups of strangers or intact leadership teams, the processes of slowing down and listening more fully and deeply means that people hear things from others that they would ordinarily miss. As the research has shown, mindfulness helps people notice and step back from default responses such as biases and stereotypes. I've seen management teams "see" one of their members as if meeting a new person with a whole range of previously overlooked contributions. I've also seen people share profound things about themselves with others who are strangers, a process which often ushers in for both parties a deep appreciation of the common humanity, and common experiences.

Further, leaders often tell me that an impact of mindfulness is a reconnection with family. Children notice that they have their dad's attention in a way they've got used to not having. Children remark that their parents are smiling more, get home earlier and listen to them. Often participants will sign up to do some classes on meditation, yoga or pilates with their partner. For me this is often one of the most satisfying pieces of feedback about the impact of mindfulness. As a facilitator of these processes, there is sometimes a very quiet, almost stunned air about groups working on mindfulness. It is as if they are remembering or reconnecting with a way of being that they'd lost sight of but have now glimpsed and feel they can retrieve.

While many of the observations above are based on anecdotal experience, there is an increasing amount of leadership research, which also documents the impact on work, and workplaces of leaders who demonstrate some of the mindful qualities we've explored here. These include the impacts of leaders who are able to gain perspective on and intervene purposefully in the action; leaders who by being wholly present make different possibilities available to those around them; and leaders who can focus their attention on what matters, initiating difficult but powerful dialogue.

Ellen Langer, Professor of Psychology at Harvard University, writes: "In more than 30 years of research, we've found that increasing mindfulness increases charisma and productivity, decreases burnout and accidents, and increases creativity, memory, attention, positive affect, health, and even longevity. When mindful we can take advantages of opportunities and avert the dangers that don't yet exist."

The emotional states of leaders significantly impact their team and their ability to face the diverse challenges as mentioned above. Therefore, one expects a strong correlation between the emotional intelligence of leaders and their mindfulness. Goleman defines emotional intelligent leaders as "people … who know and manage their own feelings well, and who read and deal effectively with other people's feelings." He echoes the work of Peter Salovey and John Mayer in defining five domains of emotional intelligence: Knowing one's emotions (self awareness); managing emotions; motivating oneself; recognizing emotions in others (empathy); and handling relationships. A mindful leader is always aware of the present moment and is able to observe it without judgment. In that given moment, he or she is therefore able to clearly comprehend the emotions of the self as well as of others. This helps mindful leaders manage their emotions and those of others better and with empathy and compassion.

In tough economic times, there's often a knee-jerk reactive argument for panic, pessimism and "getting tough" most of which generate a culture of fear. Mindfulness, practiced extensively in organizations, can be a powerful antidote to the fear and aggression tendencies. Buddhist trained HR executive, Michael Carroll, author of *The Mindful Leader: Awakening Your Natural Management Skills through Mindfulness Meditation*, applies the key principles of mindfulness and how they could apply to leaders of organizations. He argues that mindfulness in leaders and their organizations can:

- Heal toxic workplace cultures where anxiety and stress impede creativity
- Cultivate courage and confidence in spite of workplace difficulties in economic downturns
- Pursue organizational goals without neglecting the here and now
- Lead with wisdom and gentleness, not only with ambition, relentless drive and power
- Develop innate leadership talents

For leaders to become self-aware, they need to understand their life stories, and reflect on how their life stories and crucibles contribute to their motivations and their behaviors. Leaders who do not take time for introspection and reflection on their life stories and experiences are more vulnerable to being overly influenced by external rewards such as power, money, and recognition. These leaders also may feel a need to appear so perfect to others that they cannot admit vulnerabilities and acknowledge their mistakes.

Leaders learn to accept their weaknesses, failures, and vulnerabilities, just as they appreciate their strengths and successes. In so doing, they gain compassion for themselves and the ability to relate to the world around them in authentic ways. This frees them from the need to adopt pretenses to impress other people.

Leaders with low EQ often lack self-compassion. Without self-compassion, it is difficult to feel compassion and empathy for others. These leaders have a tendency to use or manipulate other people, particularly those with less perceived power. As a result, they are unable to establish authentic relationships that can be sustained over time. Leaders who develop self-awareness and self-compassion are better able to cope with high levels of stress and pressure. They maintain the capacity to empower people to perform at a very high level even under very difficult circumstances.

If we've reached a tipping point in workplace leadership it's because a new generation of workers has arrived on the scene that simply won't tolerate a work environment that fails to support them and their needs. Said another way, organizations will be unable to attract and retain this young talent if they don't adopt far more authentically supportive management practices. Gen Y's or the Millennials' impact on influencing major changes to workplace leadership is just being felt – and it only will get stronger in ensuing decades as they grow older and inevitably assume senior manager and, ultimately, CEO roles.

Collectively, Millennials have very different values than their predecessors. They're highly self-confident, very concerned about the well-being of others and group oriented. But here's what's most important. To these young workers, money is far less important. Instead, they have a strong desire to find meaning through their work.

How Mindful Leaders Incorporate the Elements of Mindfulness

Element	Leadership Behaviors
Being Present	• At meetings restrict use of mobile phones so people can focus on the present • Prior to meetings and discussions, meditate quietly on the leader's intentions • Restrain the impulse to rush through discussions to get on with the next meeting or event • Avoid overscheduling meetings • Engage in the practice of having the leader and other participants in meetings/discussions "check in" with how they are feeling • Encourage others and engage in active and empathetic listening • Structure reflection, quiet and "do nothing" times for self and employees • Create "quiet time" spaces for employees to meditate, have downtime, and nap during working hours
Paying Attention	• Restrict practices of multitasking • In meetings, practice seeking clarification and understanding different perspectives before

	responding • Encourage informal practices that reinforce one's and others' ability to focus attention
Openness	• Structure meetings and discussions that encourage a healthy receptivity to different perspectives • Practice "beginners' mind" and curiosity • Approach people with an open heart as well as an open mind
Acceptance	• Accept one's feelings and emotions without judgment without trying to block or evade them • Accept others' feelings and emotions without judgment or automatic reactivity • Separate the reality of how emotions can drive behavior • Separate behavior from judgment of character
Non-reactivity	• Understand how unconscious emotional reactions can control behavior of self and others • Learn and master emotional regulation so that the cognitive brain can balance emotional reactivity • Learn how to intentionally respond rather than unconsciously react • Understand and recognize one's emotional triggers
Compassion	• Demonstrate and practice empathy and compassion for employees and colleagues, rather than criticism and judgment, particularly when mistakes or failures occur • Practice self-compassion when mistakes or failures occur rather than engaging in mistakes or failures • Embrace social responsibility as an equal obligation to financial success for the organization • Practice one's and encourage others to practice gratitude for success and the good things
Non-attachment	• Resist the temptation to be rigidly attached to outcomes based upon past experiences • Have positive expectations without having things to look and be a certain way • Be open to a variety of possible outcomes

What Do Mindful Leaders Do Differently?

Based upon my experience in coaching senior executives in organizations combined with my examination of research, I've come to the following conclusions about how mindful leaders differ from other leaders. They:

- Personally engage in an in-depth process of self-awareness and self management and encourage others to do the same
- Learn and demonstrate a capacity for intentional response to external events rather than unconscious, "autopilot" reactivity
- Let go of their belief in themselves as technical and problem solving geniuses and embrace the notion of becoming mindful partners. This requires building an awareness of and becoming more open to nuance and subtlety
- Are open to the concept of an unknown future and uncertainty
- Are flexible enough to make changes quickly without defending their territory or ego
- Become skilled at leading through intuitive reflection rather than logical analysis
- Understand what motivates other people, particularly those from different backgrounds
- Practice attunement—listen empathetically and attentively and think about how others feel
- Practice kindness, empathy and compassion towards others in the organization, and see these behaviors as strengths, not weaknesses
- Develop a corporate culture that includes gratitude, and forgiveness for mistakes
- Demonstrate a willingness to explore and express their own feelings and emotions;
- Demonstrate vulnerability as a strength
- Are humble, rather than being driven by hubris or narcissism
- Become more open and accepting of the world and others, and their differing points of view, rather than trying to reshape the world in their own image
- Create a conversational space where all were welcome; all views were valued and people were free to explore
- Are open to others' emotions and venting without feeling threatened
- Are adept facilitators who help others gain self-awareness;
- Exhibit extraordinary curiosity and patience
- Tolerate ambivalence, ambiguity and conflict, reduce frustration, and ward off unwholesome thoughts and feelings and resist the urge to force the situation

- Incorporate into their working schedules substantial time for quiet reflection and a state of "being" in touch with their inner mental and emotional state, rather than the constant external state of "doing"
- Embrace the beliefs that "less is more," and that slowing down actually improves productivity, rather than the reverse
- Organize workplace systems and structures to incorporate mindful practices for employees—such as meetings, "quiet time" communication systems, and conflict resolution
- Model mindfulness practices for employees and customers to see.

Summary of Key Points:
- There is a crisis of confidence in leadership in organizations
- Most leaders who have failed have done so because of hubris and deficits in self awareness and emotional self management, not because of technical skills
- Leadership development programs in the past have largely been unsuccessful and not appropriate for the new economy and workplace because they excessively focus on external factors rather than the individual inner development of leaders
- Mindfulness practices have been shown to be an effective way for leaders to not only handle the modern stresses of the workplace, but improve employee engagement and productivity
- There is a clear connection among the concepts and practices of transformational leadership, emotional intelligence and mindful leadership.

To get more specific strategies for mindful leadership including a tailor-made coaching program, go to my website: http://raywilliams.ca

8 MINDFULNESS IN THE WORKPLACE

The concept of mindfulness – awareness and observation of the present moment without reactivity or judgment – has gone mainstream. A Google database search on the term mindfulness yielded more than six million links; mindfulness and work generated 1.4 million links. Amazon.com lists more than 2,000 books with mindfulness in the title or as a keyword. A PsycInfo database search produced 2,221 articles, books, and dissertations with mindfulness as a keyword.

Mindfulness Training For Employees Is A Cost Effective Strategy For Dealing With Stress

More than three decades of scientific research around the world has demonstrated that mindfulness-based stress reduction can positively, effectively, and often profoundly, reduce psychological distress. Additionally, such stress reduction and workplace studies have indicated that staffs become more resilient, productive and happier.

Initiatives to introduce mindfulness into the workplace holds a promise for a cost effective way to improve employee productivity and well-being, while reducing health care costs, most of which are stress related. In my work with CEOs, senior executives, business owners and professionals, mindfulness is a key part of their leadership training and coaching experience. And the results have been significant.

Researchers from the Schools of Medicine at Duke University and the University of Pennsylvania argue that "in order for stress management programs to be effective, they have to be accessible, convenient, and engaging to the employees," as well as cost-effective and economically sustainable for the organization. These same researchers conducted a randomized controlled trial examining the effectiveness of therapeutic yoga and mindfulness-based stress reduction programs in reducing stress, enhancing emotional well-being and work performance.

The trial enrolled 239 employee volunteers who were randomly assigned to one of three interventions: yoga, mindfulness meditation, or a control condition that provided the participants with a list of insurance-provided resources (fitness center discounts, wellness coaching opportunities). They found that compared to the control condition, the therapeutic yoga and mindfulness based programs both led to significant improvements in perceived stress levels and reduction in sleep problems, suggesting these strategies are viable interventions to implement in the workplace.

The ratio of investing in Mindfulness training has been found to be 1.0 to 5.0 according to a study by Tage Sondersgaard Kristensen of Corporate Based Mindfulness Training IF Insurance, based in the Netherlands. He observed a 19% decrease in stress, 37% increase in productivity, 40% increase in focus, 34% increase in emotional control and 37% decrease in overwhelm. Stephanie Tate's study with a Fortune 500 knowledge workforce found participants in 6-9 week course experience a 42% stress reduction, improvement in productivity, time management and job satisfaction.

Research That Supports The Effectiveness of Mindfulness Meditation In The Workplace

A large number of research studies have shown that employees who practice mindfulness meditation in the workplace were able to:

- **Separate the ego from events, experiences, thoughts and emotions more successfully.** When the ego is separated from events, negative events are decoupled from the self and become less threatening. For example, before an important presentation, the presenter might interpret thoughts about what could go wrong or potential failure as "just those nerves talking" rather than as a valid indication of inadequacy or potential failure
- **Decrease the automaticity of mental processes in which past experiences, and cognitive habits constrained their thinking**. Employees may find themselves responding to colleagues without really listening to the conversation because they believe they already know where the conversation is going. They may complete a task without recalling actually doing it or head to the store to get groceries and end up in the parking lot at work, all because of deeply ingrained, automatic responses. This is known as autopilot or mindlessness

- **Improve their behavioral response flexibility.** Response flexibility can be defined as the ability to pause before taking verbal or physical action. Response flexibility occurs when one is able to pause before responding to an environmental stimulus. A slowing down and deeper consideration of the situation before responding to workplace events and interactions characterize response flexibility. Allowing time and space to reflect and consider multiple, non-automatic ways of responding offers more opportunities for optimal outcomes and functioning. Rather than responding to workplace events habitually and invariantly, response flexibility allows one the power to act in alignment with one's goals, needs, and values
- **Develop response flexibility through the nonreactive, non-judging aspects that characterize decreased automatic reactivity.** Through decreased automaticity, individuals recognize that thoughts and reactions to an event are not an objective reality requiring immediate alteration or response. As such, the range and optimization of possible behavioral responses grows. In the workplace, increased response flexibility would contribute to a more productive environment in a variety of ways including fewer instances of escalating conflict and aggression in response to perceived threats and disagreements as well as improved decision making because reactive decision making would be less likely
- **Engage in less rumination.** When individuals are confronted with events that would normally provoke negative thought patterns, a mindful orientation makes them less likely to engage in rumination, which is a repetitive and passive focus on symptoms, causes, and consequences of distress. Rumination can "trap" one in a spiral of negative and unproductive thoughts. In a mindful state, individuals are aware of their thoughts, but can observe them and avoid evaluating their thoughts as good or bad. Individuals who engage in ruminating thought patterns are at greater risk for poor concentration, depressed mood, low self-efficacy, and are more likely to alienate those who might provide social support. Conversely, individuals who are less prone to rumination after stressful events report fewer work-related health complaints. A reduction in rumination resulting from mindfulness will have broad ranging effects on employees' performance and well-being, via improved confidence, better problem solving, more effective use of social support mechanisms, and better concentration. In addition, a reduction in rumination will lead to faster recovery from negative workplace events

- **Increase in the capacity for empathy and compassion.**
Empathy is the ability to see life from another's perspective.
Empathy allows us to be attuned to others, to resonate with them,
and to have compassion, which allows us to be sensitive to the
suffering of another, and a desire to do something about it.
Through empathy and compassion, individuals are able to consider
the larger social picture, moving out of "survival mode" by
considering what actions are best for others. Mindful empathy and
compassion is linked to decreased automaticity and increased
physiological awareness and regulation. Indeed, it is difficult for
individuals to be aware of others' perspectives if they are unaware
of their own. In essence, nonjudgmental, present-moment
awareness of one's own internal thoughts facilitates empathy and
compassion for the internal states of others

- **Develop greater emotional regulation comprising the
reduction of negative emotions as well as the generation and
maintenance of positive emotions.** Mindfulness has been linked
to generating positive emotions, reducing negative emotions when
they arise. Specifically, enhanced left prefrontal activation seems to
be a critical trigger of positive emotion, approach motivation, and
increased ability to modulate negative moods arising from the firing
of the limbic system. In terms of the influence of mindfulness on
positive emotions, meta- analytic evidence indicates a positive
association between mindfulness and positive mood states. In
other words, a cycle of positivity may develop through
mindfulness, as individuals are more likely to notice positive events
in their lives and thus experience more positive moods. The
regulation and reduction of negative emotion also has clear
implications for employee functioning. For example, individuals
who experience chronically negative mood states are more likely to
be victimized at work and to be perpetrators of workplace
aggression. And leaders' negative mood states have been linked to
followers' moods and group processing effects as well

- **Develop a connection between mindful states and feelings of
autonomy, a key component of self-determination.**
Additionally, the detached observation developed in mindfulness
training allows greater recognition of what is valued, and increased
likelihood that individuals will choose behaviors in alignment with
those values. The reduced automaticity associated with mindfulness
leads individuals to reflectively choose what has previously been
reflexively adopted or ultimately create greater congruence between
values and actions, which is at the heart of self- determined
behavior. Because mindful individuals better understand their goals

and values, and act more congruently with them, their intentions are better predictors of their behavior. Mindfulness also reduces the extent to which people see barriers to goal accomplishment, or obstacles in goal pursuit, as indications of their competency. Challenges often trigger derailing negative, self-critical, reactive, and judgmental thoughts. As individuals attempt to avoid dealing with these challenging threats to self, persistence lags. By allowing negative thoughts to occur without judgment and reaction, the thoughts and concomitant frustration dissipate, allowing successful goal pursuit. Empirical evidence has supported the notion that mindfulness plays a significant role in persistence. The implications for increased self-determination and persistence at work are broad reaching

- **Improve working memory in work settings.** Working memory or the cognitive mechanism that allows us to keep a limited amount of information active for a limited period of time plays a key role in self-regulatory processes because it is used to manage cognitive demands. The existing literature has provided considerable evidence that highly stressful or demanding situations deplete working memory capacity, partly because stressful or other physiologically and emotionally activated situations cause the adrenal glands to release stress hormones (e.g., cortisol) to meet situational demands. Although helpful in activating response systems, elevated cortisol levels in stressful situations have the unfortunate consequence of inhibiting working memory. When individuals become more aware of their bodily states, they are more able to regulate their levels of physiological activation and responses to negative thoughts and emotions. Consequently, unhealthy stress hormone production is reduced, allowing working memory to function more effectively

- **Facilitate the quality of interpersonal connections.** Mindfulness training may be related to greater social connectedness. This sense of connection may be important for the workplace as individuals higher in social connectedness tend to display more desirable interpersonal behaviors than those lower in social connectedness. In many ways, positive inter-personal relationships are a critical determinant of optimal organizational functioning , thereby underscoring the important role of mindfulness in work relationships.

Organizations That Have Incorporated Mindfulness Practices

Since mindfulness meditation has gone mainstream, an increasing number of organizations have instituted and expanded these practices for employees. Here's a partial list of them:

Google	Deutsche Bank
Proctor and Gamble	General Mills
Apple	McKinsey and Company
Aetna	U.S. Marines
Abbott Laboratories	Goldman Sachs
American Red Cross	AOL Time Warner
Comcast	EBay
General Motors	Green Mountain Coffee Roasters
Lucent International	Prentice Hall
Reebok	Starbucks
Toyota	Unilever
Xerox	Volvo
Yahoo	

I've had the pleasure to work in several organizations that have been working on instituting mindfulness practices. Invariably, the impetus comes from the CEO or senior management, although HR also is involved. In one large organization that I can speak about, the initiative came about as a result of the CEO and President of the company having gone through a considerable program of self-growth with a focus on self-awareness, self-management, and changing his style of leadership from breakneck speed to slowing down, reflection and mindfulness. His whole demeanor changed and was infectious with employees in the company. He then initiated training program for employees over a period of three years. The ambiance and feeling in the company is very different now, and there is a palatable sense of calm and caring. For those interested in bringing mindfulness into their organizations, I can suggest that without either the support or participation of senior management, you will experience limited success.

A Model For Instituting Mindfulness In The Workplace
The seven elements of mindfulness provides a ready-made model for implementing mindfulness in the workplace and can comprise both the formal process of meditation and informal mindfulness practices. An example is provided following.

Element	Employee Behaviors To Enhance Mindfulness
Being Present	<ul><li>Avoiding over analysis of events in the past</li><li>Focusing on actions that can be taken in the present moment</li><li>Avoiding excessive thinking/discussion about future events</li><li>Encouraging and practicing "savoring," pleasant activities and successes in the present</li><li>Practicing "real time" present positive feedback for performance</li><li>Not rewarding multitasking behavior</li></ul>
Paying Attention	<ul><li>Restricting the practices of multi-tasking</li><li>In meetings and conversations encouraging and emphasizing active listening before responding</li><li>Encouraging employees to take regular "unplugged" periods of quiet reflection</li><li>Training employees and encouraging them to focus attention on routine and ordinary activities (eg.walking to work, driving, entering office)</li></ul>
Openness	<ul><li>Training and encouraging employees to see each event and experience with "beginner's mind" and curiosity</li><li>Developing attitudes and perspectives that what worked in the past won't necessarily work in the present or future</li><li>Encouraging and training employees to be less judgmental</li><li>Encouraging and practicing compassion and empathy in all relationships</li><li>Being open to mistakes as opportunities for learning</li></ul>
Non-reactivity	<ul><li>Training and encouraging employees to pause and reflect before "reacting" to events or people</li><li>Training and encouraging employees to rationally and intentionally respond to events and people via their Prefrontal Cortex rather than their protective and defensive primitive brains</li></ul>
Acceptance	<ul><li>Training and encouraging employees to accept events that have already occurred (the past) rather than spending energy in denial or trying to change the past</li><li>Training and encouraging employees to be</li></ul>

		accepting and less judgmental of the feelings and emotions they may be experiencing in stressful situations (particularly if it leads to self-judgment or guilt)
		• Training and encouraging employees to resist trying to be perfectionists and refrain from self-criticism
		• Training and encouraging employees to focus on what actions can be taken based in the present moving forward
Compassion		• Training and encouraging employees to act with empathy and compassion for others
		• Training and encouraging employees to practice self compassion
		• Developing organizational programs of social responsibility
		• Expanding the organization's purpose beyond shareholder value
Non-attachment		• Encouraging employees to move beyond a "fixed mindset" of seeing things as having to be certain way
		• Encouraging employees to develop more open perspectives on possible outcomes and futures
		• Avoiding a slavish devotion to set-in-stone purposes, mission, goals and objectives

Ways in Which The Workplace Can Be Restructured To Incorporate Mindfulness

There's a multitude of ways in which workplace structures, systems and practices can easily incorporate mindfulness practices, which have been shown by research to be effective, and are incredibly cost effective. These practices are not so much things to be added or the typical reorganizational or change management efforts, but rather a different way of viewing productivity, valuing people, and embracing the importance of quiet, reflection, "doing nothing," focusing attention, being present focused, building emotional self-regulation and setting positive intentions for any activity.

Here's a practical list of mindfulness practices that are being and could be implemented:

1. Provide mindfulness meditation instruction for all employees.
2. Provide a quiet, meditation room or space for employees to access at any time during the workday.
3. Begin every meeting with a one or two minute grounding positive meditation.
4. Provide training for employees in "empathetic listening", who require being more open-minded and open-hearted.
5. Encouraging employees to take mini-mindful meditation breaks at their desk during the day.
6. Discourage employees from eating their meals at their desk while they are engaged in work.
7. Teach employees on how to "tune into" distractions around them rather than trying to block them out.
8. Teach employees how to practice "strategic acceptance". When you get stressed out and start thinking of every little setback in catastrophic terms, your mind tends to accept this black-and-white thinking as the absolute truth, which creates even more stress. But really, this thinking is just a product of your emotional reaction to a situation. When you find your stress levels rising, don't try to force yourself to cheer up or calm down. The first step to returning to equilibrium is to simply accept the way you currently feel. If you accept that that is how you feel at this moment, you take the sting out of your emotion, and out of the stress, anger, worry and unhappiness. The act of observation and the act of accepting the situation is tremendously powerful. But this doesn't mean resigning to a bad situation at work -- it's a matter of accepting how things are at this moment before making a plan to do what you can to improve them.
9. Schedule more frequent, shorter breaks from work. Research has shown that shorter blocks of work time interspersed with quiet, uninterrupted breaks, improves productivity and creativity.
10. Control multitasking. This means both having controls over the volume and frequency of emails and texting. There is overwhelming research to show that effective multitasking is a myth, and it damages productivity.
11. Teaching and encouraging employees to mindfully ground themselves before every face to face and telephone conversation.
12. Teaching and implementing positive conflict resolution skills which focus on "moving toward" difficulties and dealing with them in a mindful manner rather than avoiding them.
13. Teaching employees the mindset and skill of intentionally responding to difficult situations and people, rather than unconsciously and automatically "reacting" to them. Reactive

behavior is ruled by the unconscious and more primitive parts of our brain, whereas intentional responses rely upon the rational prefrontal cortex, a conscious activity. This requires acquiring the skill of being the observer of your emotions and pausing before any action is taken, allowing the rational part of your brain to "catch up".

14. Teaching and encouraging employees to "notice" more in their environment by being fully attentive to what is being said, including body language and nuances, empathetic listening, openness and spending less time "talking your story", or trying to be right.

15. Encouraging employees to regularly "unplug" from digital devices, even for short periods of time, to allow their brains to be involved in integration, daydreaming and reflection.

16. Encouraging employees to regularly change their environment during their lunch breaks, preferably to somewhere that is quiet and peaceful.

17. Institute workplace practices that demonstrate compassion and empathy and kindness for each other.

18. Institute more tolerance for "mistakes" without punishment or judgment. There is more than adequate research to show that mistakes and failure are the greatest teachers.

19. Teaching employees how to "pause and reflect" in a decision-making, and incorporate that practice into decision-making organizational systems.

Summary of Key Points:

- Mindfulness practices have been shown to be an effective way to help organizations reduce employee stress, and increase productivity, engagement and well-being

- Employers and leaders can easily introduce both physical changes (eg. a quiet or meditation room), formal structures and processes (eg. how meetings and conversations are held) and training initiatives (eg. meditation, yoga, tai chi) which are cost effective

- Mindfulness practices are more than just add-ons to existing professional or personal development programs. They are a different way of perceiving and experiencing work and life.

9 CONCLUSIONS

Mindfulness has gone mainstream. If you're still thinking this is merely a touchy-feely trend practiced by yogis, creatives and the business elite – you're way behind. Thousands of people in organizations around the world are now benefiting from the improved performance, communication, relationships and self-mastery that mindfulness brings. More than 40 universities now offer mindfulness in medicine training. Mindful schools have touched over 300,000 students in 43 countries. Law schools are in on it. Even the U.S. Special Forces has a mind-fitness training program.

Being mindful is more than an idea, it's a way of being, a way of living. Mindfulness recognizes and cultivates the best of who we are as human beings. The simple act of being mindful has the power to change everything — how we approach our challenges, our relationships, our communities, and ourselves.

Mindfulness is available to us because we already have the capacity to be present, and it doesn't require us to change who we are. It takes many shapes and goes by many names: attention, awareness, empathy, compassion, being in the zone, situational awareness, presence, flow, contemplation, and many more.

We can cultivate these innate qualities with simple mindfulness practices that are scientifically demonstrated to benefit ourselves — and through our relationships— our loved ones, our friends and neighbors, our co-workers, and the world at large. Being mindful is becoming part of the spirit of the times. It's helping us to become healthier, to lead more effectively, and to cooperate with each other in making a better world.

Because leaders have lost credibility in our institutions; because leaders face an increasingly more difficult and stressful job; and because workers experience more stressful and uncertain lives, with a cost to them and employers of reduced engagement and well-being, the time is right to bring mindfulness into the workplace in a cost effective and dynamic way. I encourage current and potential leaders and employee organizations to step up and seize this opportunity to make work life different and more rewarding.

To get an additional wealth of material to support the information in this book, go to my website: http://raywilliams.ca

REFERENCES

Altman, D. (2010). *The mindfulness code: Keys for overcoming stress, anxiety, fear, and unhappiness.* Novato, CA: New World Library.

Anderson, A.K. (2007). Attending to the present: mindfulness meditation reveals distinct neural modes of self-reference. *Scan*, 2, 313–322.

Aquino, K., Grover, S. L., Bradfield, M., & Allen, D. G. (1999). The effects of negative affectivity, hierarchical status, and self-determination on workplace victimization. *Academy of Management Journal*, 42, 260–272.

Avolio, A.J. et al., A meta-analytic review of leadership impact research: Experimental and quasi-experimental studies. *The Leadership Quarterly*, 20 (2009), pp. 764–784.

Azagba, S., & Sharaf, M. (2011). The effect of job stress," *Heath Economics Review*, 2: 15, 22-29.

Baer, R. A., Smith, G. T., & Allen, K. B. (2004). Assessment of mindfulness by self-report: The Kentucky Inventory of Mindfulness Skills. *Assessment*, 11, 191–206.

Barker, J. (1993). *Paradigms: The Business of Discovering the Future.* New York: HarperBusiness.

Bass R (2009) *The Bass Handbook of Leadership: Theory, Research, and Managerial Applications.* New York: Free Press.

Begley, S. (2008). *Train your mind, change your brain.* New York: Random House.

Bersin, J., & Schwartz, J. (2014). *Global Human Capital Trends 2014* Report. Deloitte Consulting.

Bishop, S.R., Lau, M., Shapiro, S., Carlson, L., Anderson, N.D., Carmody, J., Segal, Z.V., Speca, M., Velting, D. & Devins, G. (2004). Mindfulness: A proposed operational definition. *Clinical Psychology: Science and Practice*, 11 (3), 230-241.

Boyatzis, R., & McKee, A. (2005). *Resonant leadership*. Boston, MA: Harvard Business School Press.

Boyatzis, R. (2011) Neuroscience and leadership: The promise of insights. *Ivey Business Journal* (Jan/Feb).

Brantley, J., & Millstine, W. (2007). *Five good minutes at work: 100 mindful practices to help you relieve stress and bring your best to work*. Oakland, CA: New Harbinger Publications.

Brown, K. W., & Ryan, R. M. (2003). The benefits of being present: Mindfulness and its role in psychological well-being. *Journal of Personality and Social Psychology*, 84, 822–848.

Brown, K. W., Ryan, R. M., & Creswell, J. D. (2007). Mindfulness: Theoretical foundations and evidence for its salutary effects. *Psychological Inquiry*, 18, 211–237.

Bono, J. E., & Judge, T. A. (2003). Self-concordance at work: Toward understanding the motivational effects of transformational leaders. *Academy of Management Journal*, 46, 554–571.

Branham, L. (2005). *The 7 Hidden Reasons Employees Leave*. New York: AMACOM Books.

Burns, James MacGregor. (1979). *Leadership*. New York: Harper Collins.

Campbell, M., et al. (2007). *The Stress of Leadership*. Center for Creative Leadership White Paper.

Carroll, M. (2006). *Awake at work: 35 practical Buddhist principles for discovering clarity and balance in the midst of work's chaos* (2nd ed.). Boston: Shambhala.

Carroll, M. (2007). *The Mindful Leader: Ten principles for bringing out the best in ourselves and others*. Boston, Trumpeter.

Cashman, K. (2008). *Leadership From The Inside Out: Becoming a Leader For Life*. San Francisco: Berrett-Kohler.

Chambers, R., Gullone, E., & Allen, N. B. (2009). Mindful emotion regulation: An integrative review. *Clinical Psychology Review*, 29, 560–572.

Chambers, R., Lo, B. C. Y., & Allen, N. B. (2008). The impact of intensive mindfulness training on attentional control, cognitive style, and affect. *Cognitive Therapy and Research*, 32, 303–322.

Chemers, M. (1997). *An Integrative Theory of Leadership*. New York: Psychology Press.

Chatzisarantis, N. L. D., & Hagger, M. S. (2007). Mindfulness and the intention-behavior relationship within the theory of planned behavior. *Personality and Social Psychology Bulletin*, 33, 663–676.

Chiesa, A., & Serretti, A. (2009). Mindfulness-based stress reduction for stress management in healthy people: A review and meta-analysis. *Journal of Alternative and Complementary Medicine*, 15, 593–600.

Chiesa, A., & Serretti, A. (2010). A systematic review of neurobiological and clinical features of mindfulness meditations. *Psychological Medicine: A Journal of Research in Psychiatry and the Allied Sciences*, 40, 1239–1252.

Church, A. H. (1997). Managerial self-awareness in high-performing individuals in organizations. *Journal of Applied Psychology, 82*, 281–292.

Clawson, J. G. (2006). *Level Three Leadership: getting below the surface.* PrenticeHall, Upper Saddle River, New Jersey.

Cohen, J. S., & Miller, L. J. (2009). Interpersonal mindfulness training for well-being: A pilot study with psychology graduate students. *Teachers College Record*, 111, 2760–2774.

Christensen, C., & Van Buren, D. (2013). Consulting on the cusp of disruption. *Harvard Business Review*, 12, 26-32.

Csikszentmihalyi, M. (1990). *Flow: the psychology of optimal experience.* New York, US: HarperCollins.

Davidson, R. J. (2010). Empirical explorations of mindfulness: Conceptual and methodological conundrums. *Emotion*, 10, 8–11.

Deloitte (2015). *The Deloitte Millennial Survey, 2015.* Deloitte.

Denning, S. Has Capitalism reached a turning point. *Forbes* magazine, September 26, 2013.

Desbordes et. al. (2012). Effects of mindful-attention and compassion meditation training on amygdala response to emotional stimuli in an ordinary, non-meditative state. *Frontiers of Human Neuroscience*, 6, 26-39.

Dickman, M.H., and Stanford-Blair, N. (2009). *Mindful Leadership: A Brain-Based Framework.* Thousand Oaks, CA.: Corwin Press.

Dotlich, D. (2003). *Why CEO's Fail: The 11 Behaviors That Can Derail Your Climb to the Top and How to Manage Them.* San Francisco, CA.: Jossey-Bass.

Dueck, C. (2007). *Mindset: The New Psychology of Success.* New York: Ballantine.

Dutton, K. (2013). *The Wisdom of Psychopaths.* Toronto: Anchor Books.

Edgar, C. (2009). *Inner Productivity: A Mindful Path to Efficiency and Enjoyment in Your Work.* New York: Cruzado Press.

Eurich, T. (2013). *Bankable Leadership: Happy People, Bottom-Line Results, and the Power to Deliver Both.* New York: Greenleaf Books.

Finkelstein, S. (2004). *Why Smart Executives Fail: And What You Can Learn from Their Mistakes.* New York: Penguin.

Galinsky, E., et al., (2004). *Overwork in America.* Families and Work Institute Report.

Germer, C. K. (2005). Mindfulness: What is it? What does it matter? In: C. K. Germer, R.D. Siegel Giluk, T. L. (2009). Mindfulness, Big Five personality, and affect: A meta-analysis. *Personality and Individual Differences*, 47, 805–811.

George, B. (2010). Leadership's Lost Decade. Wall Street Journal February 3, 2010.

Goldstein, J., & Kornfield, J. (2001). *Seeking the Heart of Wisdom: The Path of Insight Meditation* . Boston: Shambhala.

Goleman, D. (1995)*Emotional Intelligence*. New York: Bantam Dell.

Goleman, D., & Boyatzis, R. (2013). *Primal Leadership, With a New Preface by the Authors: Unleashing the Power of Emotional Intelligence*. Cambridge, MA.: Harvard Business Review Press.

Goleman, D., Boyatzis, R., & McKee, A. (2001). Primal Leadership: The Hidden Driver of Great Performance. *Harvard Business Review* 79(11), 42-51.

Gonzalez, M. (2012). *Mindful Leadership: The 9 Ways To Self Awareness, Transforming Yourself and Inspiring Others*. San Francisco: Jossey-Bass.

Gunaratana, H. (2002). *Mindfulness in Plain English* (Revised and Expanded ed.). Boston: Wisdom.

Hall. L. (2013). *Mindful Coaching: How Mindfulness Can Transform Coaching Practice*. London, UK: Kogan Page.

Hamel, G. The End of Management. *The Wall Street Journal*, August 21, 2010.

Hanh, T. N. (1976), *The miracle of mindfulness*, Boston, Beacon Press.

Hassed, C. (2008). Mindfulness, well-being and performance. *NeuroLeadership Journal*, 1, 1-7.

Harter, J.,& K.; Schmidt, F. Well-being in the workplace and its relationship to business outcomes: A review of the Gallup studies. In Keyes, C., & M. Keyes, C.L. (Eds.).*Flourishing: Positive psychology and the life well-lived*. Washington, D.C.: American Psychological Association.

Hanson, R. (with R. Mendius). 2009. *Buddha's Brain: The Practical Neuroscience of Happiness, Love, and Wisdom*. New Harbinger.

Hölzel, B. K., S. W. Lazar, et al., (2011). "How does mindfulness meditation work? Proposing mechanisms of action from a conceptual and neural perspective." *Perspectives on Psychological Science* 6(6): 537-559.

Hout, T. (1999). *Are Managers Obsolete?* Cambridge, MA.:Harvard Business Review Press

Jha, A., & van Vugt, M. (2011). Investigating the impact of mindfulness meditation on training on working memory. *Cognitive Affective Behavioral Neuroscience*, 11 (3), 344-353.

Kabat-Zinn, J. (2007). *Arriving at your own door: 108 lessons in mindfulness*. New York: Hyperion Press.

Kabat-Zinn, J. (1994). *Wherever you go there you are: Mindfulness meditation in everyday life*. New York: Hyperion Press.

Kabat-Zinn, J. (2005). Coming to our senses: Healing ourselves and the world through mindfulness. New York, NY: Hyperion.

Korn, M. Managing Mental Health At Work. *Wall Street Journal.* August 28, 2012.

Kouzes, J. M., & Posner, B. Z. 1995. *The leadership challenge: How to keep getting extraordinary things done in organizations.* San Francisco, CA: Jossey-Bass.

Langer, E. J. (1989a). *Mindfulness.* Reading, MA: Addison-Wesley.

Langer, E. J. (1989b). Minding matters: The consequences of mindlessness-mindfulness. *Advances in Experimental Social Psychology,* 22, 137–173.

Lieberman, M. (2013) *Social: Why Our Brains Are Wired to Connect.* New York: Crown.

Love, A. & Maloney, J. (2009). Mindfulness as capacity: at the threshold of leadership's next wave? *NeuroLeadership Journal,* 2, 1-7.

Lutz, A., Slagter, H. A., Dunne, J. D., & Davidson, R. J. (2008). Attention regulation and monitoring in meditation. *Trends in Cognitive Sciences,* 12, 163–169.

Martin, R. (2011). CEOs must model the behavior for creating societal value. *Harvard Business Review,* 9, 26.

Marturano, J. (2013). *Finding The Space To Lead.* New York: Bloomsbury:

Mindfulnet. (2011). Mindfulness in the workplace. Available at http://www.mindfulnet.org/ page9.htm. Retrieved on February 23, 2011.

Moses, B. (2009). *What Next: Find the Work That's Right For You.* Toronto: Doring Kingsley.

Nakai, P., & Schultz, R. (2000). *The Mindful Corporation: Liberating the Human Spirit at Work.* Long Beach, California: Leadership Press.

Neff, K. (2011). *Self-Compassion: Stop Beating Yourself Up and Leave Behind.* New York: HarperCollins.

Pfeffer, J. (1998). *The Human Equation.* Cambridge: Harvard Business Review Press.

Pfeffer. J. & Fong, C. (2004). *The Business School 'Business.* Stanford University Working Paper No 1855,

Pillay, S.S. (2011). *Your brain and business: The neuroscience of great leaders.* New Jersey, US: Pearson Education Inc.

Psfk. (2014). *The Future of Work: A PSFK Labs Report.* PSFK Labs.

PWC. (2014). *The Future of Work—The Journey To 2022.* PWC

Rock, D. (2008). SCARF: a brain-based model for collaborating with and influencing others. *NeuroLeadership Journal,* 1, 1-9.

Rock, D. (2006). *Quiet Leadership: Six Steps To Transforming Performance At Work.* New York: Harper Collins.

Rock, D.,& Schwarz, J. (2006). The neuroscience of leadership. *Strategy+Business,* 43, 1-6.

Rousmaniere, D. A Futurist looks at the future of marketing. *Harvard Business Review,* May 24, 2013.

Schwartz, A. The Future of Work. *Co-Exist.* March 2013.

Seppala, E. *20 scientific reasons to start meditating today. Psychology Today,* September 11, 2013.

Sears, S., & Kraus, S. (2009). I think therefore I am: Cognitive distortions and coping style as mediators for the effects of mindfulness meditation on anxiety, positive and negative affect, and hope. *Journal of Clinical Psychology,* 65, 561–573.

Shapiro, S. L., Carlson, L. E., Astin, J. A., & Freedman, B. (2006). *Mechanisms of mindfulness. Journal of Clinical Psychology,* 62, 373–386.

Sherman, H., & Shulz, R. (1999). *Open Boundaries: Creating Business Innovation Through Complexity.* New York: Basic Books.

Siegel, D. J. (2007). *The mindful brain: Reflection and attunement in the cultivation of well-being.* New York: Norton.

Siegel, D. J. (2010). *Mindsight: The new science of personal transformation.* New York: Bantam.

Siegel, R. D., Germer, C. K., & Olendzki, A. (2009). Mindfulness: What is it? Where did it come from? In: F. Didonna (Ed.), *Clinical handbook of mindfulness* (pp. 17–35). New York: Springer.

Sisbee, D. 2004).*The Mindful Coach: Seven Roles For Helping People Grow.* Marshall, N.C.: Ivy River Press

Siegel, R.D. (2010). *The Mindfulness Solution: Everyday Practices For Everyday Problems.* New York: The Guilford Press.

Solis, B. (2011). *The End of Business As Usual: Rewire the Way You Work to Succeed in the Consumer Revolution.* New York: Wiley.

Taylor, K. Why Millennials Are Ending The 9 to 5. *Forbes,* August 23, 2013.

Tan, C-M. (2012). *Search Inside Yourself: The Unexpected Path To Achieving Success, Happiness (And World Peace).* New York: Harper Collins.

Tang, Y.Y., Ma, Y., Wang, J., Fan Y., Feng, S., Lu, Q., Yu, Q., Sui, D., Rothbart, M.K., Fan, M. & Posner, M.I. (2007). Short-term meditation training improves attention and self-regulation. *National Academy of Sciences of the United States of America,* 104, (43) 17152-17156.

Tipsord, J. (2009). The effects of mindfulness training and individual difference in mindfulness on social perception and empathy. *Unpublished doctoral dissertation,* University of Oregon, Portland, OR.

Treadway, M. T., & Lazar, S. W. (2009). The neurobiology of mindfulness. In: F. Didonna (Ed.), *Clinical handbook of mindfulness* (pp. 45–57). New York: Springer.

Valentine, E., & Sweet, P. (1999), "Meditation and attention: A comparison of the effects of concentrative and mindfulness meditation on sustained attention", *Mental Health, Religion and Culture.* 2(1), 59–70.

Weber Shandwick (2013). *Civility In America: A Nationwide Survey.*

Weick, K. E., & Putnam, T. (2006). Organizing for mindfulness: Eastern wisdom and Western knowledge. *Journal of Management Inquiry*, 15, 275–287.

Weick, K. E., & Sutcliffe, K. M. (2006). Mindfulness and the quality of organizational attention. *Organization Science*, 17, 514–524.

Williams, J. M. G. (2010). Mindfulness and psychological process. *Emotion*, 10, 1–7.

Williams, M. and Penman, D. (2011). *Mindfulness: An Eight-Week Plan For Finding Peace In A Frantic World*. New York: Rodale.

Williams, Ray (1992). *The Leadership Edge*. Vancouver: EduServ.

Williams, Ray (2007). *Breaking Bad Habits*. Vancouver: Ocean Publications.

Whitmyer, C. (Ed.). (1994). *Mindfulness and Meaningful Work: Explorations in Right Livelihood*. Berkeley, California: Parallax Press.

Workplace Bullying Institute (2014). *2013 WBI U.S. Workplace Bullying Survey*.

Wren, J.T. (1995) *The Leader's Companion: Insights On Leadership Through The Ages*. New York: The Free Press.

Zeidan, F., et al. (2012). Mindfulness meditation improves cognition: Evidence of brief mental training. *Consciousness and Cognition*, 12, 2, 597-605.

ABOUT THE AUTHOR

Ray Williams is owner and President of Ray Williams Associates, a Vancouver based company providing executive coaching, leadership training and speaking services.

Ray's undergraduate and graduate training has been History, English, Organizational Psychology, Human Performance and Leadership/Management. He brings over 35 years experience to his clients as a CEO, senior HR executive and consultant. Ray is a certified master executive coach and certified professional speaker. He is widely regarded as one of Canada's top executive coaches.

Ray is the recipient of the Master Educator Award from the American Society of Education Executives, and is also past President of the International Coach Federation in Vancouver and Governor of the National Staff Development Council in the U.S. As an educator he was co-founder of the Olympics of the Mind Program for students in Canada. He has clients in Fortune 500 companies, Best Managed Companies in Canada and small to medium sized businesses and non-profit organizations throughout the world in the areas of leadership, workplace culture, team development and peak performance. He has been very active in such organizations as the Vancouver Board of Trade, having recently served as Director and Vice-Chair, and other professional and community service organizations.

Ray has written for or been interviewed by *The Washington Post, Forbes, USA Today, NBC News, The Huffington Post, Entrepreneur, MacLean's, American Business Journal, The Financial Post, Fast Company, Psychology Today, Salon,* and dozens of other and other national and international publications having published more than 300 articles. He has written a book on leadership, *The Leadership Edge,* a personal growth book, *Breaking Bad Habits,* and was contributing author to *Systemic Change,* and the Best Seller, *Ready, Aim, Influence.*

Ray is in high demand as an executive coach, leadership trainer, mentor, relationships expert, platform speaker, workshop presenter and facilitator throughout North America. He brings a varied life experience of living in several countries throughout the world, and understands cultural diversity and differing perspectives. His unique experience of having survived a POW camp in WWII as a prisoner of the Japanese has also enabled him to understand and assist his clients in overcoming obstacles and handling stress.

Ray can be reached at ray@raywilliamsassociates.com or through his website at http://raywilliams.ca

Made in the USA
Charleston, SC
15 October 2016